Middle East Security Issues

In the Shadow of Weapons of Mass Destruction Proliferation

Editor

BARRY R. SCHNEIDER

Air University Press
Maxwell Air Force Base, Alabama

December 1999

Library of Congress Cataloging-in-Publication Data

Middle East security issues: in the shadow of weapons of mass destruction prolifera-
tion/Barry R. Schneider, editor.
    p. c.m

    1. Middle East—Strategic aspects. 2.Weapons of mass destruction—Middle East.
3. National security—Middle East. 4. United States—Military policy. I. Schneider,
Barry R.

    UA832.M5225 1999
    355'.033056—dc21   99-0588978

Disclaimer

Contents

Chapter   Page

DISCLAIMER   ii

PREFACE   v

1   NBC and Missile Proliferation Issues
     in the Middle East   1
     Lawrence Scheinman

2   Recent Military Developments in the
     Persian Gulf   27
     Anthony H. Cordesman

3   Arab Perspectives on Middle Eastern
     Security   61
     Ibrahim A. Karawan

4   Regional Security and Arms Control in the
     Middle East: The Nuclear Dimension   77
     Avner Cohen

5   The Egyptian-Israeli Confrontation over the
     Nuclear Nonproliferation Treaty   109
     W. Andrew Terrill

CONTRIBUTORS   135

Preface

The Middle East is an international flashpoint, a place where open warfare could erupt at any time. It is the home of numerous countries possessing some combination of weapons of mass destruction (WMD) (nuclear, biological, or chemical weapons), and is an area where states are developing an increasing capability to deliver such WMD by missiles and/or aircraft. The Middle East is also the home of US friends who oppose each other as well as rogue states who are hostile to the United States. In short, the Middle East is a WMD war waiting to happen. Such a conflict would harm US allies and US interests; it needs to be avoided. Or, if WMD warfare occurs, such a conflict needs to be limited and the United States and allied forces need to be prepared to cope with the effects.

The authors of this study address important questions that demand an answer if US national security policy is to be well informed. In chapter 1, "NBC and Missile Proliferation in the Middle East," Dr. Lawrence Scheinman, director of the Washington, D.C., office of the Monterey Institute of International Studies, summarizes the nuclear, biological, and chemical weapons capabilities and missile systems of Egypt, Iran, Iraq, Israel, Libya, and Syria. He sees the region as one of the most tension-ridden, conflict-prone and heavily armed regions of the world. He addresses the questions of what the various state players have, why they have it, and what this implies for the stability of the region. He notes that WMD has already been used repeatedly in the region. For example, Egypt, Syria, Iraq, and Iran have used chemical weapons against their adversaries. Iran and Iraq from 1980–88 engaged in the first two-way ballistic missile war in history. As the range of delivery systems increases, and as warheads are loaded with more lethal payloads, the situation will become more threatening should warfare be renewed in the region. Scheinman argues that while the United States and its allies need an effective deterrent and defense capability (counterproliferation), he believes that stability is best served by universal adherence to, and compliance with treaties to prevent the proliferation of WMD.

The second chapter, "Recent Developments in the Persian Gulf," by Anthony H. Cordesman, senior fellow at the Center for Strategy and International Studies in Washington, D.C., looks at both the conventional and WMD military balance between the states in the region. This chapter looks at the volume of arms transfers to each state in the region and the impact on its military capacity and the balance of power. He evaluates the conventional military capability of regional powers vis-á-vis each other and when pitted against the United States. Cordesman believes that the key wild card or unknown about the region is the possible use of WMD to trump the conventional advantages of an adversary. Military outcomes may be a function of how high up the escalation ladder each side is willing to climb and how much risk each will entertain in future crises or conflicts.

Chapter 3, "Arab Perspectives on Middle Eastern Security," is written by Dr. Ibrahim A. Karawan, the associate director of the Middle East Center at the University of Utah. He concludes that "the fact that the Middle East has not been among the success stories in curbing the spread of nuclear weapons is not surprising." He believes that policy makers in the surrounding Arab and Muslim states cannot ignore the fact of Israeli nuclear weapons and explains the proliferation of chemical and biological weapons in such states as a natural deterrence response. Karawan addresses the differing Arab and Israeli approaches to arms control in the region, and rejects the Israeli case for maintaining the sole WMD deterrent and outlines the differences in approach to sequencing and priorities in inching toward a Middle East WMD-free zone. Karawan indicates that a growing number of Arab states have realized the futility of any strategy that relies on military power against Israel, a significant alteration of Arab policy that once reelected the three noes: no peace, no recognition, and no negotiations with Israel. Dr. Karawan addresses the question of whether nuclear proliferation in the region would likely lead to greater stability or instability and he concludes it will not. This drives him to the conclusion that there is no better alternative to peace and stability in the region than to try to bring about a negotiated NWFZ in the Middle East, however unrealistic that may seem at present.

Chapter 4 is on the same subject from the perspective of an independent Israeli analyst, Avner Cohen, author of the well-regarded book, *Israel and the Bomb* . Cohen sees a long-term trend in the Arab world to accept Israeli existence and see it as a state with which the Arabs must deal. Cohen explains the two diametrically opposite approaches taken by the two sides in the Arms Control and Regional Security (ACRS) negotiations, the universalist versus the regional approach to the problems of WMD disarmament in the area. Cohen also addresses the problem of who should be included before a NWFZ is to be negotiated, signed, and ratified. He addresses the usefulness of the proposal to halt the production of fissile material for nuclear weapons and the impact on the Middle East if each state were to embrace the Fissile Material Cutoff Treaty. He also addresses the possible utility of virtual weapons as a means of moving the sides to embrace a WMD free zone. Virtual weapons would be defined as the memory and capability of building new nuclear, biological, or chemical weapons if one side were to be discovered cheating on the agreement. So long as states have scientists who know how to design, test, assemble, and deploy new WMD, perhaps, he speculates, their political leaders might be willing to forego the real thing one day. Cohen asserts that the future of nuclear arms control in the region will depend on two broader developments, progress toward the settlement of the Arab-Israeli conflict and the evolution of politics and society in states outside the region.

Chapter 5, by Dr. W. Andrew Terrill, associate of the US Air Force Counterproliferation Center and senior international security analyst at Lawrence Livermore National Laboratory, focuses more narrowly on "The Egyptian-Israeli Confrontation over the Nuclear Nonproliferation Treaty." Dr. Terrill contrasts Egypt's changing approach to the Israeli nuclear weapons possession, alternatively ignoring it and then challenging it. Like Cohen, Terrill also compares and contrasts the Egyptian and Israeli views of how best to accomplish a Middle East nuclear-free zone or WMD-free zone. He also details the ups and downs of the Middle East peace negotiations and the

ACRS process in the post-Rabin era. Neither side, he concludes, is prepared to concede that the other has correctly framed the question of how to move forward toward a more stable region free of nuclear arms or other WMD. Until the sides can agree on a process, peace and nuclear disarmament will be elusive.

This volume originated as a symposium at the US Air War College in August 1998 when the five participants spoke to the class and faculty at Maxwell AFB. This symposium was part of the core course directed by Dr. George Stein, chairman of the Department of Future Conflict Studies at the Air War College.

Thanks are due to Mr. Michael Yaffe, formerly of the US Arms Control and Disarmament Agency, now employed by the Department of State and to Dr. Steven Speigel of the UCLA Center for International Relations for funding the speakers and writers of this project. The USAF Counterproliferation Center also thanks Col Thomas D. Miller and his staff at HQ USAF/XONP, as well as Mr. Vayl Oxford and Col Thomas Hopkins of the Defense Threat Reduction Agency for their continued support that enabled us to pay for printing, copy editing, and distributing this volume.

Barry R. Schneider
Director
USAF Counterproliferation Center

Chapter 1

NBC and Missile Proliferation Issues in the Middle East

Lawrence Scheinman

The conviction that the proliferation   of nuclear and other weapons of mass destruction (WMD) presents grave threats to national security, international stability, and civilized society has led the majority of states to take steps to prevent the further spread of such weapons and to create the basis and conditions for their elimination from the arsenals of all states. States have negotiated and brought into force treaties and conventions dealing with nuclear, biological, and toxin weap - ons, and chemical weapons. The means of delivery of such weapons, in particular, missiles, have also been a subject of attention, resulting in the establishment of a voluntary ar - rangement among key supplier states to control the transfer of certain unmanned delivery systems and the equipment and technology that could contribute to their production.

The Nonproliferation Treaty of Nuclear Weapons (NPT) which came into force in 1970 has the largest number of adherents of any arms control treaty in history (186) with only four states in the international system still not parties—Cuba, Israel, In - dia, and Pakistan. The NPT is designed to prevent the spread of nuclear weapons, to provide assurance through safeguards applied by the International Atomic Energy Agency (IAEA) that peaceful nuclear activities in nonnuclear weapon states will not be diverted to weapons purposes, and to promote peaceful uses of nuclear energy. While the NPT makes a distinction between nonnuclear weapon states and nuclear weapon states (defined as states that manufactured and exploded a nuclear weapon or other nuclear explosive device prior to 1 January 1967), it does not outlaw nuclear weapons but contains the only formal obligation to end the nuclear arms race and to negotiate toward achieving nuclear disarmament.

The 1975 Biological and Toxin Weapon Convention (BTWC) and the 1997 Chemical Weapons Convention (CWC) go further than the NPT. They are global treaties that ban an entire class

1

of WMD; make no distinction between have and have-not states; bind all parties not to develop, produce, stockpile, or acquire the covered agents; and prohibit the use or preparation of such weapons. One hundred forty-two states have ratified or acceded to the BTWC and an additional 18 have signed but not yet ratified. One hundred sixty-nine states have signed the CWC, of which 117 had ratified or acceded by the end of 1998.

The Missile Technology and Control Regime   (MTCR) was formed in 1987 among eight states including the United   States and its G-7 partners to restrict transfers of nuclear-capable missiles and related technology. The agreement includes guidelines and an annex of items subject to control. Missiles covered by the regime include any capable of delivering a   500-kilogram or greater payload a distance of 300 kilometers or more that is to say, payloads and distances relevant to local - ized conflicts such as the Middle East. Twenty-eight states now participate in the regime which now covers unmanned delivery systems capable of carrying all types of WMD. Other states that are not formal members have adhered to the MTCR guidelines on a voluntary basis. China has agreed to abide by the parameters of the regime but has not accepted the annex controlling missile technology and component exports. North Korea is completely outside the regime and exports a range of missiles and capabilities that undermines efforts to control proliferation.

Increasing numbers of states look to these treaties, conven- tions, and regimes to provide a framework for an environment supportive of their political and security objectives. For exam- ple, 50 states have adhered to the NPT since the beginning of the decade, bringing this treaty to the brink of universal ac - ceptance. The indefinite extension of this treaty in 1995 made it a permanent part of the international security architecture. The majority of the international community has a strong pref- erence for a world in which nuclear weapons play a progres - sively diminished role and ultimately disappear. Continued growth in support for CWC and BTWC, including efforts in the latter case to strengthen its verification provisions, reflects simi- lar judgments regarding the WMD covered by those agreements.

If the weight of international opinion leans heavily toward the view that more proliferation   is worse, not all agree, as demonstrated in the two regions which are home to states that have refused to join the NPT—South Asia (India and Pakistan) and the Middle East (Israel). This raises the question of why states might choose to acquire nuclear weapons (or other WMD) or the capability to produce them and to resist adhering to agreements that would create legally binding obligations not to proliferate. This question also applies to states such as Iraq and North Korea, who joined the NPT but then violated their agreement. One or more of three explanations—national secu - rity; global or regional status and prestige; and domestic po - litical reasons including bureaucratic, technocratic, and mili - tary-industrial politics—usually account for national decisions on whether to join and comply with nonproliferation treaties and regimes. All three explanations could apply to India's de - cision to conduct a series of nuclear tests in May 1998, but security and status rather than domestic politics would seem to account more fully for WMD decisions in the Middle East.

The Middle East is one of the most tension-ridden, conflict-prone and heavily armed regions in the world. The Arab-Israeli conflict has been the most prominent and dangerous conflict in the second half of the twentieth century because it is due to the nonacceptance of the legitimacy of the Israeli state and wars aimed at its annihilation. Although there has been con - siderable progress as reflected in the conclusion of peace trea-ties between Israel and its Egyptian and Jordanian neighbors, and progress with the Palestinians through the Middle East peace process, not all important states in the region have accepted this trend (for example, Iran and Iraq) and, as recent events demonstrate, the overall situation remains fragile. That, however, is only one of a number of regional conflicts driven by history, ethnicity, religion, politics, and territorial disputes that have placed Arab against Arab, Iraq against Iran, and Iran against the presence of outside influence in the Persian Gulf.

For more than 30 years, the Middle East has been a region of concern with regard to nuclear weapons and recently with regard to chemical and biological weapons. Chemical and bio - logical weapons are seen as easier to acquire than nuclear weapons and highly lethal. Middle Eastern governments have also shown increased interest in and have acquired greater access to missile delivery systems with expanded ranges. On top of this, the Middle East continues to be the world's largest recipient of conventional weapons. As costs for these conven-tional weapons continue to rise exponentially, pressure to ac-quire WMD will also mount.[1]

Given the massive conventional threat to its survival, Israel chose to create a nuclear infrastructure that would enable it to access nuclear weapons if security conditions dictated. At the same time it maintained a posture of nuclear ambiguity claiming that it would not be the first to introduce nuclear weapons into the region. The policy of deliberate ambiguity was almost certainly adopted out of concern for the political costs and consequences to US-Israeli relations. Israel was concerned about the complications that could result for that relationship, in particular US conventional arms transfers and close defense ties, given the strong and public US commit-ment to the NPT and to its universal acceptance. It also re-flected an Israeli assessment that an open declaration of nu-clear status would not strengthen Israel's security, but might create significant pressure in neighboring states to follow Is-rael down the nuclear path. An unleashing of a nuclear arms race in the region would not be in Israel's interest. Israel's position on nuclear ambiguity has not altered over the years. Although in the wake of the South Asian nuclear tests and Iran's flight testing of a long-range missile (Shahab-3, based on the North Korean Nodong-1, which has a 1,000- to 1,300-kilometer range), it is reported that the government apparently has begun a review of its policy of nuclear ambiguity.[2]

Iraq is the other Middle East state to have made a major effort to establish a nuclear capability. Unlike Israel, it pur-sued this objective while a party to the NPT and under obliga-tion not to "manufacture or otherwise acquire nuclear weap-ons or other nuclear explosive devices; and not to seek or receive any assistance in the manufacture" of same. Iraq's motivations reach beyond security concerns engendered by its geopolitical proximity to its larger competitive neighbor, Iran, to its political ambitions, which include asserting itself as leader and spokesman for the Arab world. This pits it against Egypt, which traditionally has seen itself in that role. Iraq also as-pires to be the dominant if not hegemonic power in the en ergy-rich Persian Gulf. This aspiration ensures continued tension and conflict with Iran, which is the other aspirant. United Nations Special Commission (UNSCOM) and IAEA operations inside Iraq revealed major programs to acquire not only nu - clear but also chemical and biological weapons and their means of delivery in an effort to establish a formidable and potentially irresistible force that could compel the behavior of other states in the region and deny outside powers the ability to intervene effectively to prevent Iraq from achieving its goals. Reflecting on behavior like this, one Israeli scholar concluded that "in the Middle East, war is still seen as a primary instru - ment of policy and for many states such as Iraq, Libya or Iran, limitations and global regimes (such as NPT, CWC, BTWC) are marginal obstacles to be overcome, or . . . simply ignored."[3]

Against this background, one must evaluate Iranian motiva tions and objectives vis-á-vis WMD. In many ways what is said of Iraq can be said for Iran. As described by Shahram Chubin,

> (T)he parallels . . . between these two states are important. . . . Iran and Iraq border on one another and have experienced war and defeat; they harbor resentments and grievances; they are ambitious regionally, which pits them against Israel; and they are hostile to the West, particularly the United States, and its presence in the Gulf. . . . In the near term, the key variables affecting the proliferation of weapons of mass destruction . . . will be the lessons drawn from recent events, . . . the availability of resources and access to suppliers, and the costs and penalties incurred by clandestine WMD programs. In the longer term, the evolution of Arab-Israeli relations, the stability and orientation of the [Gulf Cooperation Council] states, and the future of the regimes in Iran and Iraq will be important factors as well. *Even without Israel, Iraq and Iran would have each other as principal justifications for pursuit of WMD capabilities.* (Emphasis added)[4]

This last point deserves emphasis. Having been victimized by Iraqi use of chemical weapons during one Gulf war and subjected to punishing missile attacks in the "war on the cities" phase of that conflict, Iran determined not to be caught short again and to equip itself to deter and defend against future contingencies in which WMD might play a role. This theme was underscored by Hashemi Rafsanjani prior to be - coming president in asserting to the Iranian parliament that "with regard to chemical, bacteriological and radiological weapons . . . it was made very clear during the war that these weapons are very decisive. . . . We should fully equip ourselves in the defensive and offensive use of (these) weapons."[5]

However, while security-related experience clearly plays a significant role in Iranian thinking about WMD, broader con - siderations are also relevant. As Chubin also notes, "As a revo- lutionary state intent on spreading its values and increasing its influence, Iran may consider nuclear weapons the weapons of choice. Both as a deterrent against its enemies and as a means of amplifying its voice internationally, nuclear weapons may appear tailor-made for the regime [which] is motivated more by its view of the world and Iran's role, as opposed to the country's geopolitical context or domestic political structure."[6]

Israel, Iraq, and the revolutionary nature of the Iranian re - gime are factors in Teheran's thinking. There is also the pres - ence of a radical regime on Iran's eastern borders (Afghani - stan), opposition to it in the Gulf states, and its proximity to South Asia where two states have carried out nuclear tests and have moved from undeclared to declared status in the nuclear realm.

Syrian motivations for WMD appear to be less grandiose and more focused on security-specific concerns which include not only Israel, with whom it has territorial disputes (the Go - lan Heights), but, in the longer run, also Iraq and Turkey. Earlier assumptions about an allied Syrian-Egyptian military challenge to Israel disappeared two decades ago at the Camp David Accords with the shift in Egyptian policy toward Israel, and with the end of the cold war and demise of the Soviet Union. This resulted in the attrition of support Damascus had been receiving from Moscow. Syria does not at present appear to have aspirations or infrastructure to be a nuclear weapon state and does not have a program that would enable it to establish capability to go down the nuclear path. It has a significant chemical weapons capability including a large stockpile of chemical agents and weapons as well as missiles capable of delivering these weapons deep in Israeli territory. With no articulated doctrine for use of such weapons, one must surmise that they are intended as a deterrent against either an overwhelming Israeli conventional attack or a nu - clear threat.

Libya is more difficult to assess. Although it has no signifi - cant nuclear infrastructure, it has a history of interest in acquiring nuclear weapons, including efforts to buy them and offering lucrative rewards to nuclear scientists and techni - cians to work on Libya's behalf. Its flamboyant leader, Muam - mar Qadhafi, has for more than a decade made declarations urging Arab states to acquire nuclear weapons. In 1987, for example, Qadhafi stated that "we should be like the Chi - nese—poor and riding donkeys, but respected and possessing an atom bomb."[7] A decade later, in January 1996, he made the more pointed statement that "the Arabs who are threatened by the Israeli nuclear weapons have the right to try in any way possible to possess these weapons so that a balance is achieved and so that the region is not left at the mercy of the Israelis."[8] The first statement appeals to the prestige of having nuclear weapons and fits in with the pan-Arabist thrust of Qadhafi's policies. The second statement addresses the secu - rity implications of not having nuclear weapons not only vis-á- vis Israel, but also in relation to the United States, with which Libya has been in confrontation due to its support for terrorist activities abroad and its efforts to acquire WMD. Libya has not made headway in developing a nuclear infrastructure or capa- bility, and instead has placed emphasis on more easily acces - sible chemical weapons. There is a belief that Libya has manu - factured chemical weapons in large numbers using agents produced in a domestic facility at Rabat, as well as having established a research and development program for biological agents. Its alleged use of chemical weapons against neighbor - ing Chad in the mid-1980s suggests that for Libya such weap- ons have operational utility and are more than deterrents. Libya also maintains a missile development program that de - pends heavily on outside assistance. Progress in missile devel- opment has become difficult since the UN embargo on the transfer of missile components and technologies to Tripoli.

Egypt appears to have given up its nuclear weapons aspira- tion since the mid-1970s following its defeat in the 1973 war with Israel. It has focused instead on building up its conven - tional capabilities. It has not given up all interest in WMD which may be seen as a hedge against Israeli nuclear capabil - ity and, equally likely, as important to its claims as spokes -

7

man for an Arab world. Egypt has had chemical weapons for three decades, using them in North Yemen three times in the 1960s. It is presumed to maintain some capability to produce them if needed. Egypt has refused to sign the Chemical Weapons Convention until Israel makes concessions on the nuclear issue in the context of the Arms Control and Regional Security (ACRS) talks that are part of the Middle East Peace Process (MEPP).

Progress in ACRS has been nonexistent largely due to a deadlock between Egypt and Israel over how to proceed with arms control. Egypt has insisted that the process begin with Israeli concessions on the nuclear issue by acceding to the NPT or moving ahead toward establishing a nuclear-weapon-free zone (NWFZ) in the region, or some other significant concessionary move in the nuclear arena. Israel sees the resolution of nuclear-related issues as something to be achieved in the context of a just, lasting, and comprehensive peace. ACRS provides a beginning, not an end, since four states (Syria, Libya, Iraq, and Iran) are hostile to Israel and are not participants in ACRS. Egypt 's frustration with its failure to move Israel on nuclear issues is compounded by its inability thus far to get any satisfaction on the resolution adopted at the 1995 NPT Review and Extension Conference . This resolution called upon states in the Middle East "to take practical steps in appropriate forums aimed at making progress towards, inter alia, the establishment of an effectively verifiable Middle East zone free of WMD, nuclear, chemical and biological, and their delivery systems."[9] Some analysts in Cairo have questioned whether Egypt's position on the NPT ought to be reassessed in light of the stalemate on nuclear dialogue, a question, which if answered positively, could have a profoundly negative impact on regional stability, not to speak of the nonproliferation regime itself.

Against this background, what is the status of WMD in the Middle East today? The tables in the appendix describe the situation as of 1998 for all WMD and delivery systems, both manned and unmanned, in the six states covered in this chapter. What is evident from the tables is that with the exception of Iran, none of the states in the region have joined all three treaties related to WMD. There is no common obligation or commitment against proliferation. Unlike the other five states, Israel is not a party to the NPT. Only Iran has signed and ratified the CWC. While all except Israel have signed the BTWC, Syria and Egypt have not ratified it and Iraq ratified it only because it was required to do so as part of the Gulf War cease-fire terms. Not being party to the NPT, Israel is not subject to the scrutiny of the IAEA safeguards system. The Arab states, having not signed, and Israel having signed but not ratified the CWC, are not subject to verification that they do not possess and are not producing or stockpiling prohibited or controlled chemical agents. This means in both the NPT and CWC cases that an important confidence-building measure based on monitoring, transparency, and corroboration of in - formation through independent verification is lacking.

The risk of proliferation in the region has not abated, and in some cases activity related to WMD has intensified. All states in the region are involved in one way or another in activities related to WMD. Nuclear programs or related activities exist in Iran, Israel, and Iraq. In Iraq , the nuclear program forged in the decade before the Gulf War was uncovered and destroyed or dismantled pursuant to UN Security Council resolutions. But uncertainty persists whether all aspects of that program including nuclear weapon components relevant to triggering a nuclear explosion, have been acknowledged and accounted for, and whether the nuclear file on Iraq should be closed and efforts focused on implementing the less intrusive long-term monitoring and verification regime called for by the Security Council. The basis for reconstituting a weapons program—the human infrastructure of trained scientists and engineers—re - mains intact and so does the political will. In the view of two experts on the Iraqi program, "Iraq could make a nuclear device within two to twelve months after deciding to do so, assuming it acquired sufficient fissile material."[10] Iraq contin - ues to prevent further UNSCOM inspections. Experts believe that Iraq could reconstitute its biological, chemical, and mis - sile capabilities in less than a year.

Iran's incipient nuclear program does not pose an imminent risk of proliferation but is a potential long-term threat. Iran's emphasis is on completion of the Bushehr power reactor . Iran also has sought to acquire fuel cycle capabilities including a heavy water research reactor, a uranium conversion plant, uranium enrichment equipment, maraging steel, and ring magnets as well as other technologies and equipment not crucial to a purely civilian power reactor program but that could be relevant for a nuclear weapons program. Taking this into consideration along with earlier rhetoric from Iranian leadership and the situation in Iraq and Iran-Iraq relations, many are led to conclude that the ultimate objective is acquisition of nuclear weapons. In other areas of WMD, Iran appears to focus on acquiring materials, equipment, and technology to support and grow its capabilities. It has continued to seek equipment and technology to support a more advanced infrastructure for chemical warfare. It has been reported that Iran was seeking to recruit scientists who had worked on the So viet biological weapons program.[11]

Significantly, Iran appears to be focused on increasing self-sufficiency by acquiring indigenous production capability. This is especially true in the case of medium-range ballistic missiles to complement its existing capacity to produce short-range missiles. The recent Shahab-3 test attested that Iran is rapidly approaching the ability to indigenously produce mis - siles with ranges that bring much of the region under threat. Generally, the more self-sufficient and less dependent on ex - ternal sources of supply a state becomes, especially one that is politically and diplomatically isolated, the less opportunity others may have to exercise influence and restraint on the state, making the situation even more problematic than before.

The same pattern (but not necessarily with the same result) seems to describe activities in Syria, Libya, and Egypt . These activities include on-going research and in some cases devel - opment programs in chemical and biological weapons, espe - cially with regard to ballistic missiles. Egypt has a continuing relationship in the ballistic missile field with North Korea; Libya seeks the same relationship in both chemical warfare and ballistic missiles; and this is also true for Syria.

In short, all countries in the region have active development or procurement programs cutting across the different kinds of WMD and in particular with respect to delivery systems. Al - though the MTCR export control system has limited and slowed the pace of acquisition of missile capabilities, missile proliferation is moving steadily ahead in all of the countries concerned. Insofar as the acquisition of missiles serves as an added driver for acquisition of WMD, it becomes clear that missile proliferation is the single most destabilizing factor currently in play in the region.

One troubling aspect to all of this is the fact that both chemical weapons and missiles have been used (separately, not together) in regional confrontations in the past. As men - tioned, Egypt, Syria, Iraq, and Iran have used chemical weap - ons against their adversaries. Breaking the taboo against use of such weapons sets dangerous precedents. Potential targets of such weapons may acquire comparable weapons and capa - bilities with increased risk of threats and counterthreats of devastating retaliation. This is particularly unwelcome in a region marked by as many tensions and confrontations as the Middle East. Anthony Cordesman points out the dangers are further increased by virtue of the differences among Middle Eastern states in terms of strategy (if they have one), tactics, operations, and capabilities relating to WMD, and by the fact that these weapons are largely in the hands of political loyal - ists to regimes rather than in the hands of professional mili - tary personnel.[12]

The Middle East is a very dangerous place, at risk in terms of stability and security and the intensification of competitive proliferation in WMD and delivery systems throughout the region. With the United States' extensive and long-standing interests in the Middle East, this has serious implications. As described in the April 1966 Department of Defense report, *Proliferation: Threat and Response,* those interests include "se- curing a just, lasting and comprehensive peace between Israel and all Arab parties with which it is not yet at peace; main - taining our steadfast commitment to Israel' security; . . . build - ing and maintaining security arrangements that assure the stability of the Gulf region and unimpeded commercial access to its petroleum reserves; . . . ensuring fair access for Ameri - can business to commercial opportunities in the region; com - bating terrorism; and promoting more open political and eco - nomic systems and respect for human rights and the rule of law."[13]

A proliferated region threatens to impose limits and con -
straints on the ability of the United States to protect and
promote these interests, in particular where the projection of
military force may be involved. A nuclear-armed adversary
with ballistic missile capabilities that could threaten US forces
in the field or even US territory could have a major effect on
the decision to deploy military forces. To the extent that the
ability to intervene militarily is constrained by such considerations, the capability to support or defend US interests in the
region would be compromised. As one observer has noted, it
goes beyond capability to the question of political will: "In the
United States, proliferation is likely to sharpen the debate
about vital versus peripheral national interests, undermine
the political support for military intervention, or even long-
term engagement, increase U.S. vulnerability to coercive diplomacy by regional actors, and narrow the room for maneuver in
[the] international environment."[14] In a region where there is
no indigenous balance, if a regional power acquires the ability
to impose limits and constraints on outside powers to inter -
vene, provide balance, and protect their interests, the regional
power gains flexibility to pursue its objectives. This increases
the potential for the regional power to achieve a predominant if
not hegemonic standing which can further reduce the capacity
of an outside power to support its interests in the region.[15]

Adversaries armed with chemical or biological weapons
would likely have a limited capacity to deny the United States
an ability to project force into the region if the United States
has passive defense measures in place that would enable military forces to survive and fight through the conditions created
by such weapons.

What may hold true for the United States may not hold true
for its allies such as Israel Lacking strategic depth and having
a population that is largely concentrated in a few centers,
Israel sees itself as vulnerable. We have already noted the
impact on Israel of the Iranian test of a medium-range ballistic
missile on revisiting its own nuclear posture. A senior Israeli
official recently noted that "such missiles make no military
sense if armed with conventional high explosives (HE) war -
heads. . . . Were they to be armed, however, with chemical or
biological warheads they would become immensely effective

terror weapons against civilian targets. Were they to be armed with nuclear warheads they would irrevocably change the face of the Near East."[16]

The United States shares Israeli concerns that military ca - pabilities involving WMD in the hands of revisionist or revolu - tionary states like Iraq and Iran could change the regional balance of power. This could make future wars more indis - criminate and more costly and make US fulfillment of commit- ments to allies in the region more difficult.[17]

The Gulf War with Iraq demonstrates the problem. To carry out the military campaign to drive Iraq out of Kuwait , the United States forged a coalition including states in the region which could provide bases, staging areas, airfields, and a lo - gistical lifeline that could support the Desert Storm campaign. Whether the coalition could have been assembled if Saddam Hussein was known to have nuclear weapons is a frequently raised question, and most analysts answer no. If regional states had been unwilling to host out-of-region military forces, or to join a coalition against a state known to have nuclear weapons and the means by which to deliver them, that would have made the US ability to prosecute a decision to meet and defeat the Iraqi aggression considerably more difficult or even impossible. An inability to effectively confront the aggression would have spillover effects. In particular, it may damage the confidence of allied states in US future willingness to live up to commitments to protect them.

In sum, proliferation is a fact of life in the Middle East, driven primarily by states with strong grievances against the established order and a determination to change things to suit their vision, and responded to by those who otherwise might be victimized by the success of revisionist and revolutionary regimes. The acquisition of WMD and delivery systems, par - ticularly by states with aggressive agendas, heightens percep - tions of threat, undermines the military balance, and weakens the already precarious stability of the security environment of the Middle East. Continued proliferation has the potential to severely tax the capacity and potentially the will of the United States to act assertively in defense of its significant and long- standing interests in the region. The cost of not meeting that challenge outweighs the cost of doing so, not only in terms of

US interests in the region, but also concerning the global order. An open breakout of WMD proliferation in the Middle East would have serious and perhaps irremediable conse - quences for the nonproliferation regimes.

How should the United States deal with a situation in which the key states in a region have an incentive to acquire WMD or the means to acquire them; in which some proliferation has already occurred and the effort is increasing; and in which continuation of these patterns threatens to jeopardize the abil- ity of the United States to protect and promote its interests in the region.

It is axiomatic that there are no single answers, no simple solutions. As one observer has written, what is needed is a "comprehensive set of political, economic, military and diplo - matic policies aimed at . . . halting the spread of weapons, . . . coping with the consequences of their proliferation, shaping the will to acquire as much as the means to acquire, and working toward deproliferation where it is a serious pros - pect."[18] Effective policy to achieve this result depends on the presence and mutual reinforcement of three elements—deter - rence, defense, and regimes.

Deterrence in the form of a credible threat to retaliate against aggression involving the use of WMD remains an es - sential component of a strategy to deal with the challenge posed by states possessing these weapons. A successful deter- rence policy should have the effect of dissuading possessors of WMD from using or threatening to use them. What should be the character of that deterrence is another matter. Deterrence can be based on nuclear or other means. Having a credible capability across a spectrum of forces optimizes the potential effectiveness of deterrence; for one thing it strengthens the credibility of the threat. In the post-cold war face of adversar - ies lesser than the former Soviet Union, and a concern with threats other than nuclear, there is a question how nuclear deterrence fits in. Should it be limited strictly to deterring the use of nuclear weapons by other states (as argued for by the Canberra Commission and by the National Academy of Sci - ences [NAS] in its report on the *Future of U.S. Nuclear Weapons Policy*), or should the door be left open to the possibility that the consequences of using chemical or biological weapons could be nuclear retaliation.

Current policy is ambiguous on the point. Then-Secretary of Defense William Perry (and earlier Secretary of State James Baker in reference to possible Iraqi use of chemical weapons at the time of Desert Storm) asserted that in response to a chemi - cal weapons attack the United States would deliver ab solutely devastating and overwhelming responses. The United States has a wide range of military capabilities to make good on that threat and the total range of available weapons would be con - sidered. Since nuclear weapons are part of this range, this was taken to imply the possible expansion of the role of nu clear weapons beyond their role during the cold war. Equally strong statements have been made that the traditional mission of nuclear weapons has not expanded and that US negative se - curity assurances in the NPT and in protocols to NWFZ trea - ties are not to use or threaten to use nuclear weapons against parties to these treaties. A compelling case for deterrence of use of any WMD through an array of credible responses ap - pears to be a necessary component of a nonproliferation strat- egy.

Both active and passive defense capabilities are particularly relevant to coping with the consequences of proliferation. While nuclear deterrence may ultimately be the most compel - ling means of dealing with a nuclear threat, threats arising from chemical and biological weapons are open to a wider range of responses. Passive defense refers to capabilities to provide protection against the effects of exposure to WMD. This includes the ability to detect and identify chemical or biological agents with sufficient early warning to invoke such countermeasures as donning protective clothing or gas masks and taking medical antidotes that would negate the effects of exposure. If a country could make it clear to a would-be ag - gressor that use of such weapons would be of only limited value because of the ability to defeat their purpose through passive defense measures, the aggressor might conclude that their use would not be worth the costs. Passive defense is more feasible for military personnel than for metropolitan ci vil- ian populations unless the population was provided with pro -

tective gear and inoculated with a vaccine against such potential biological warfare agents as anthrax.

Active defenses designed to interdict WMD include missile defenses to intercept ballistic or cruise missiles (the latter being potentially useful for chemical or biological warheads), and counterforce capabilities to disable the infrastructure and command and control systems to launch WMD delivery systems. The Patriot theater missile defense system deployed in the Middle East during the Gulf War is an example of the former. The development of advanced weapons and munitions capable of penetrating protective barriers and neutralizing WMD exemplifies the latter.[19] Both active and passive forms of defense are important not only for military value when confronting an adversary armed with WMD but also for political value in bolstering the will of states to join coalitions to confront regional aggressors and to allow such out-of-region powers as the United States to use their territory for bases and staging areas.

However important deterrence and defense may be to forging effective strategies for dealing with threats by states armed with WMD, they can only provide limited or short-term responses. The strongest foundation for a strategy to deal with the proliferation threat is universal adherence to, and compliance with, treaty-based regimes designed to prevent the proliferation of WMD. The regimes discussed here all contain provisions for controlling the transfer of equipment, material, and technologies that are necessary to efforts to acquire nuclear, biological, or chemical weapons and delivery systems. The more developed regimes also include means to verify compliance, thereby providing a basis for others to gain confidence in the behavior of regime parties. Regimes also provide a foundation for assembling political coalitions to deal with violations of or threats to the regime.

Regimes in this sense are denial-oriented instruments, but they also create opportunities for states to organize their relationships in given areas of responsibility—here, security—on the basis of cooperation rather than military competition. Nonproliferation regimes are arms control regimes and epitomize the aphorism that "arms control is defense by other means." In this case, verified removal of WMD from the natural competition between states takes away the most threatening and apocalyptic dimensions of that competition without sacrificing national security.

Regimes are formed where basic political preconditions relevant to their purpose have been achieved. In the Middle East, the situation is so riven with tensions that the conditions for forging consensual or contractual regimes do not exist. The global nonproliferation regimes are not seen by major players in the region as addressing their basic security requirements. Even if some players' security concerns were satisfied, other objectives served by holding WMD may not be satisfied. While these conditions limit the impact global regimes have on the behavior of some states, they do not make regimes irrelevant. Regimes provide the context for pursuing alternative ap - proaches and allow for tailored solutions and institutional arrangements. Regionally anchored regimes can be embedded in global regimes without undermining the norms and principles of the latter. Revitalizing ACRS and moving the Middle East Peace Process agenda forward are first steps in this direction.

Global regimes provide more than context. Through export control agreements and arrangements, they slow down, com - plicate, and make more costly the efforts of proliferators to acquire equipment, material, and technologies. The scope of this control has grown over time and now covers components, subcomponents, dual use equipment and technology so that those who seek to create indigenous capabilities to produce the elements of WMD find it more and more difficult to suc - ceed. Export controls buy time. The key question is what is done with that time to remove the incentives to acquire WMD. Sometimes, if the proliferation can be stalled, problems disap - pear when new political leaders emerge to change policies of states previously bent on acquiring WMD. Time used well serves the interest of nonproliferation; time used poorly only delays eventual crisis.

Global regimes also exert influence on the behavior of states that are not parties to the regimes. International relations are multifaceted and complex. State interactions involve political, economic, financial, technological, social, diplomatic, military, and other issues. This can affect, and has affected, the behavior of states. Israel has remained an undeclared nuclear-capable state. India and Pakistan did the same and justified conduct- ing nuclear tests in May 1988 on security grounds without claiming that they were going to climb all the way up the proliferation ladder. For their actions they have been paying a heavy price in the form of sanctions and embargoes. States will be reluctant to act in a contrarian manner out of concern that they may destroy important relationships. Even India, which has been most defiant of the NPT regime, has asserted that it will sign the Comprehensive Test Ban Treaty, will join in the negotiating of a Fissile Material Cutoff Treaty (both of which are critical components of the overall nonproliferation regime), and will exercise restraint with respect to its demon - strated nuclear capability.

How effective regimes will be in containing or reversing pro- liferation depends on how their members respond to noncom - pliance. The NPT does not make specific provision for dealing with noncompliance other than with respect to safeguards ap- plied by the IAEA The IAEA, upon a finding of noncompliance, can report this to the United Nations Security Council. What happens then is unclear. Iraq's invasion of Kuwait resulted in the UN Security Council taking action in the course of which the scope of Iraq's efforts in acquiring WMD became known. In January 1992 the president of the council asserted that, "the proliferation of all WMD constitutes a threat to international peace and security."[20] This phrase unlocks the door to meas - ures including the use of force. Firm commitment by the United Nations to consider any proliferation a threat to peace and security and to stand unified and firm against such events could provide the collective security measure needed to give the assurances and guarantees for their security that states seek, especially those not under the protection of an alliance or bilateral defense.

Conclusion

The Middle East remains a dangerous place. It is, as we have seen, tension ridden, conflict prone, and heavily armed and has within it some states that are either disposed or sus- ceptible to one or another form of proliferation. Political condi- tions have not evolved to the point where nonproliferation and arms control can play predominant roles in regional political-security dialogues. On the other hand, many regional political leaders have not ignored the destabilizing risks of overt proliferation of WMD to their own national security.

While deterrence and defense are more prominent features of security policies in the region, confidence-building, arms control and nonproliferation measures do have a place. Ulti - mate decisions on proliferation are the province of national political leadership. Their disposition one way or the other is a function of many and complex cross-pressures and will be largely determined by those variables. The global nonproliferation regimes now in place do not fully capture the needs of a number of these states. It is more likely that although many of the countries in question have joined one or another of the global regimes, distinctive regional solutions such as zones free of WMD, comprehensively defined and effectively verified, will play a major role in the Middle East.

Nevertheless the global nonproliferation regimes remain highly relevant. They define the expectations and affect the behavior of their members. They establish the political-legal framework for policies of denial such as export control re - gimes, and for taking national and collective economic, politi - cal, diplomatic and in some cases more forceful measures against proliferators whose behavior threatens to undermine the integrity of those regimes. They also create opportunities for individual and multinational incentives for promoting non - proliferation, for example, by addressing the legitimate secu - rity interest of states through positive and negative security assurances. They are the basis for advancing the efforts of all states to move steadily toward delegitimizing and ultimately eliminating all WMD.

Notes

1. Anthony H. Cordesman, *Weapons of Mass Destruction in the Middle East: National Efforts, War Fighting Capabilities, Weapons Lethality, Terrorism and Arms Control Implications* (Washington, D.C.: Center for Strategic and International Studies, February 1988). For an up-to-date overview of nuclear developments in the Middle East countries see also Rodney W. Jones and Mark G. McDonough in *Tracking Nuclear Proliferation:*

A Guide in Maps and Charts, 1998 (Washington, D.C.: Carnegie Endowment for International Peace, 1998).

2. Barbara Opel-Rome, *Defense News,* 14–20 September 1998, 6; and James Kitfield, *National Journal,* 1 August 1998, 1820.

3. Gerald M. Steinberg, "Israeli Arms Control Policy: Cautious Realism," *The Journal of Strategic Studies,* June 1994, 1.

4. Shahram Chubin, "Eliminating Weapons of Mass Destruction: The Persian Gulf Case," Henry L. Stimson Center, Occasional Paper, no. 33, March 1997, 2, 4. For a discussion of the broader Middle East arena in regard to weapons of mass destruction see Yair Evron, "Weapons of Mass Destruction in the Middle East," Henry L. Stimson Center, Occasional Paper, no. 39, March 1998.

5. Ibid., 9.

6. Ibid., 25.

7. Leonard S. Spector, *The Undeclared Bomb* (Cambridge, Mass.: Ballinger Publishing Co., 1988), 202.

8. Jones and McDonough, 215.

9. NPT/CONF/1995/32/RES 1 (Resolution on the Middle East).

10. David Albright and Khadhim Hamza, "Iraq's Reconstitution of its Nuclear Weapons Program," *Arms Control Today,* October 1998, 13.

11. *New York Times,* 8 December 1998.

12. Cordesman.

13. Office of Secretary of Defense, *Proliferation: Threat and Response* (Washington, D.C.: April 1996).

14. Brad Roberts, "From Nonproliferation to Antiproliferation," *International Security,* Summer 1993, 158.

15. Chubin, 1.

16. Robbie Sabel, Carnegie Endowment Conference on Non-Proliferation, January 1999.

17. Chubin, 5.

18. Roberts, 163.

19. See Office of the Secretary of Defense, *Proliferation Threat and Response,* for a detailed discussion of counterproliferation measures to complement nonproliferation.

20. United Nations Security Council Declaration on Disarmament, *Arms Control and Weapons Of Mass Destruction,* S/PV.3046, 31 January 1992.

Appendix

EGYPT

Weapons of Mass Destruction Capabilities and Programs

Nuclear	• No evidence of a weapons program. • 22MW and 2MW research reactors at Inshas, both under IAEA safeguards. • Has only engaged in basic scientific research since the 1960s. Acceded to the NPT on 2/26/81; signed the CTBT on 10/14/96.
Chemical	• Used mustard gas in Yemeni civil war, 1963–67. • Unconfirmed reports of developing nerve agent feed stock plants. • Supplied Syria with chemical weapons (CW) in early 19?0s. • Supplied Iraq with CW agents and technology during the 1980s. • Not a signatory of the CWC.
Biological	• May have a biological weapons program, though not large in scale. • Signed the BTWC on 4/10/72, but has not ratified the Convention.
Ballistic Missiles	• 100+ Scud-B with 300 kilometer (km) range and 985 kilogram (kg) payload. • Approximately 90 Project T missiles with 450km range and 985kg payload. • Developing Scud-C variant production capability with North Korean assistance, with 550km range and 500kg payload. • Developing Vector missile with 800km to 1,200km range and 450-1,000kg payload.
Cruise Missiles	• AS-5 Kelt with 400km range and 1,000kg payload. • Harpoon with 120km range and 220kg payload. • AS-1 Kennel with 100km range and 1,000kg payload. • HY-2 Silkworm with 95km range and 513kg payload. • Otomat Mk1 with 80km range and 210kg payload. • FL-I with 50km range and 513kg payload. • Exocet (AM-39) with 50km range and 165kg payload. • SS-N-2a Styx with 43km range and 513kg payload.
Other Delivery Systems	• Fighter and ground-attack aircraft include: 115 F-16C, 25 F-16A, 29 F-4E, 18 Mirage 2000C, 53 Mirage 5D/E, 20 Mirage 5E2, 42 Alpha Jet, 53 PRC J-7, 44 PRC J-6, and 74 MiG-21.

The appendices are based on the Monterey institute or International Studies project on proliferation of weapons of mass destruction in the Middle East and can be seen in complete form with extensive footnotes on the MIIS website.

	• Ground systems include artillery and rocket launchers, notably 72 FROG-7, artillery rockets with 12 launchers, which have a 70km range and carry a 450kg warhead, and 100+ SAKR-80 rockets with 12+launchers, which have an 80km range and 200kg payload.

IRAN

Weapons of Mass Destruction Capabilities and Programs

Nuclear	• Large nuclear development program to construct power reactors for civilian energy generation, reliant on Russian assistance. • 5MW and 30KW research reactors and .01KW critical assembly at Esfahan and Tehran, which are under IAEA safeguards. • US and Israeli officials believe Iran seeks to acquire the capability to build nuclear weapons. • Ratified the NPT on 2/20/70; signed the CTBT on 9/24/96.
Chemical	• Began CW production in mid-1980s, following CW attacks by Iraq. • Limited use of chemical weapons in 1984-1988 during war with Iraq, initially using captured Iraqi CW munitions. • Began stockpiling cyanogen chloride, phosgene, and mustard gas after 1985. • Reportedly initiated nerve agent production in 1994. • Ratified the Chemical Weapons Convention on 11/3/97, but has not submitted an initial declaration.
Biological	• Research effort reportedly initiated in 1980s during war with Iraq. • Suspected research laboratory at Damghan. • May have produced small quantities of agents and begun weaponization. • Ratified the BTWC on 8/22/73.
Ballistic Missiles	• Approximately 150 Scud-C with 500km range and 700kg payload. • Up to 200 Scud-B with 300km range and 985kg payload. • Approximately 25 CSS-8s with 150km range and 190kg payload. • Unknown quantity of indigenous Mushak missiles with ranges from 120km to 200km, and payloads of 150kg to 500kg. • Launched almost 100 Scud-B against Iraq during 1985-1988. • Developing Shahab-3 with over 1,000km range and over 700kg payload, and Shahab-4 with 2,000km range and 1,000kg payload.
Cruise Missiles	• HY-4/C-201 with 150km range and 500kg payload. • Harpoon with 120km range and 220kg payload. • SS-N-22 Sunburn with 110km range and 500kg payload.

	• HY-2 Silkworm with 95km range and 513kg payload. • YJ-2/C-802 with 95km range and 165kg payload. • AS-9 Kyle with 90km range and 200kg payload. • AS-11 Kilter with 50km range and 130kg payload.
Other Delivery Systems	• Ground attack and fighter aircraft include: 30 Su-24; 60 F-4D/E; 60 F-4A; 30 MiG-29; 60 F-5E/F; and 24 F-7. Most not operational due to lack of spare parts. • Ground systems include artillery and rocket launchers, notably hundreds of Oghab artillery rockets with a 45km range and unknown payload, and hundreds of Nazeat (N5) artillery rockets with a 105 – 120km range and 150kg warhead.

IRAQ

Weapons of Mass Destruction Capabilities and Programs

Nuclear	• With sufficient black-market uranium or plutonium, could fabricate a nuclear weapon within one year. • If United Nations Special Commission (UNSCOM) inspections were to be terminated, could produce weapons-grade fissile material within several years. • Retains large and experienced pool of nuclear scientists and technicians. • Retains nuclear weapons design, and may retain related components and software. • Repeatedly violated its obligations under the NPT, which it ratified on 10/29/69. • Repeatedly violated its obligations under United Nations Security Council (UNSC) Resolution 687, which mandates destruction of Iraq's nuclear weapon capabilities. • Until its termination by Coalition air attacks and UNSCOM removal programs, Iraq had an extensive nuclear weapons development program, with 10,000 personnel and a multiyear budget totaling approximately $10 billion. • In 1990, Iraq also launched a crash program to divert reactor fuel under IAEA safeguards to produce nuclear weapons.
Chemical	• May retain stockpile of chemical weapon (CW) munitions, including special chemical/biological al-Hussein ballistic missile warheads, 2,000 aerial bombs, 15,000-25,000 rockets, and 15,000 artillery shells. • Believed to possess sufficient precursor chemicals to produce hundreds of tons of mustard gas, VX, and other nerve agents. • Retains sufficient technical expertise to revive CW programs within months. • Repeatedly used CW against Iraqi Kurds in 1988 and against Iran in 1983-1988 during the Iran-Iraq war. • An extensive CW arsenal-including 33,537 munitions, 690 tons of CW agents, and over 3,000 tons of CW precursor chemicals has been destroyed by UNSCOM.

	• Repeatedly violated its obligations under UNSC Resolution 687, which mandates destruction of Iraq's chemical weapon capabilities. • Not a signatory of the Chemical Weapons Convention.
Biological	• Iraq's claim that it destroyed biological weapon (BW) munitions unilaterally including 157 R-400 aerial bombs and all of its special chemical/biological al-Hussein warheads has not been verified by UNSCOM. • May retain biological weapon sprayers for Mirage F-I aircraft. • May retain mobile production facility with capacity to produce dry biological agents (i.e., with long shelf life and optimized for dissemination). • Has not accounted for 17 tons of BW growth media. • Maintains technical expertise and equipment to resume production quickly of anthrax, botulinum toxin, aflatoxin, and Clostridium perfringens (gas gangrene). • BW prepared for missile and aircraft delivery during 1990–1991 Gulf War. • Conducted research on BW dissemination using unmanned aerial vehicles. • Repeatedly violated its obligations under UNSC Resolution 687, which mandates destruction of Iraq's biological weapon capabilities. • Ratified the BTWC on 4/18/91, as required by the Gulf War cease-fire agreement.
Ballistic Missiles	• May retain components for dozens of Scud-B and al-Hussein missiles, as well as indigenously produced Scud missile engines. • If UNSCOM inspections were to be terminated, could resume production of al-Hussein missiles within one year. • Maintains clandestine procurement network to import missile components. • Launched 331 Scud-B missiles at Iran during the Iran-Iraq war, and 189 al-Hussein missiles at Iranian cities during the 1988 "War of the Cities." • Developing Ababil-100 with 150km range and 300kg payload, flight-testing al-Samoud with 140km range and 300kg payload, and producing Ababil-50 with 50km range and 95kg payload.
Cruise Missiles	• C-601/Nisa 28 with 95km range and 513kg payload. • HY-2 Silkworm with 95km range and 513kg payload. • SS-N-2c Styx with 80km range and 513kg payload. • Exocet AM-39 with 50km range and 165kg payload. • YJ-1/C-801 with 40km range and 165kg payload.
Other Delivery Systems	• Fighter and ground attack forces include approximately 300 fixed-wing aircraft, consisting of Su-25, Su-20, Su-7, MiG-29, MiG-25, MiG-23BN, MiG-21, Mirage F1EQ5, and F-7. • Ground systems include artillery and rocket launchers, notably 500+ FROG-7 artillery rockets and 12-15 launchers, with 70km range and 450kg payload.

ISRAEL

Weapons of Mass Destruction Capabilities and Programs

Nuclear	• Sophisticated nuclear weapons program with an estimated 100-200 weapons, which can be delivered by ballistic missiles or aircraft. • Nuclear arsenal may include thermonuclear weapons. • 150MW heavy water reactor and plutonium reprocessing facility at Dimona, which are not under IAEA safeguards. • IRR-15MW research reactor at Soreq, under IAEA safeguards. • Not a signatory of the NPT; signed the CTST on 9/25/96.
Chemical	• Active weapons program, but not believed to have deployed chemical warheads on ballistic missiles. • Production capability for mustard and nerve agents. • Signed the CWC on 1/13/93, currently debating its ratification.
Biological	• Production capability and extensive research reportedly conducted at the Biological Research Institute in Ness Ziona. • No publicly confirmed evidence of production. • Not a signatory of the BTWC.
Ballistic Missiles	• Approximately 50 Jericho-2 missiles with 1,500km range and 1,000kg payload, nuclear warheads may be stored in close proximity. • Approximately 50 Jericho-1 missiles with 500km range and 500kg payload. • MGM-52 Lance missiles with 130km range and 450kg payload. • Shavit space launch vehicle (SLV) with 4,500km range and 150kg to 250kg payload. • Unconfirmed reports of Jericho-3 program under development using Shavit technologies, with a range up to 4,800km and 1,000kg payload. • Developing next (Shavit upgrade) SLV with unknown range and 300-500kg payload.
Cruise Missiles	• Harpy lethal unmanned aerial vehicle (UAV) with 500km range and unknown payload. • Delilah/STAR-1 UAV with 400km range and 50kg payload. • Gabriel-4 anti-ship cruise missile with 200km range and 500kg payload. • Harpoon anti-ship cruise missile with 120km range and 220kg payload.
Other Delivery Systems	• Fighter and ground-attack aircraft include: 2 F-151; 6 F-15D; 18 F-15C; 2 F-15B; 36 F-15A; 54 F-16D; 76 F-16C; 8 F-16B; 67 F-16A; 50 F-4E-2000; 25 F-4E; 20 Kfir C7; and 50 A-4N.

	• Ground systems include artillery and rocket launchers. Also, Popeye-3 land-attack air-launched missile with 350km range and 360kg payload, and Popeye-1 land-attack air-launched missile with 100km range and 395kg payload.

LIBYA

Weapons of Mass Destruction Capabilities and Programs

Nuclear	• Seeking to purchase or develop nuclear weapons since the early 1970s. • Nuclear scientific research program remains at rudimentary stage. • Maintains 10MW research reactor at Tajura under IAEA safeguards. • Ratified the NPT on 5/26/75, has not signed the CTBT.
Chemical	• Used small quantities of mustard agent against Chadian troops in 1987. • Produced 100+ metric tons of nerve and blister agents at Rabta facility in the 1980s. • Initiated construction of underground chemical agent production facility at Tarhunah. • Not a signatory of the Chemical Weapons Convention.
Biological	• Limited research-and-development program, but no evidence of production capability. • Ratified the BTWC on 1/19/82.
Ballistic Missiles	• Scud-C variant with 550km range and 500kg payload, 100+ Scud-B missiles with 300km range and 935kg payload. • Launched two Scud-B missiles at a US Navy base on the Italian island of Lampedusa in 1987. • SS-21 Scarab with 70km range and 480kg payload. • Program to develop al Fatah (Iltisslat) missile with 950km range and 500kg payload, under gradual development for over 15 years.
Cruise Missiles	• SS-N-2c Styx with 85km range and 513kg payload. • Otomat Mk2 with 80km range and 210kg payload. • Exocet (AM-39) with 50km range and 165kg payload.
Other Delivery Systems	• Fighter and ground attack aircraft include: 6 Su-24; 45 Su-20/22; 3 MiG-25U; 60 MiG-25; 15 MiG-23U; 40 MiG-23N; 75 MiG-23; 50 MiG-21; 15 Mirage F-1ED; 6 Mirage F-1BD; 14 Mirage F1-AD; 14 Mirage 5DD; 30 Mirage 5D/DE; and 30 J-1 Jastreb. • Bombers include 6 Tu-22.

	• Ground systems include artillery and rocket launchers, notably 144+ FROG-7 missiles and 40 launchers with 70km range and 450kg payload.

SYRIA

Weapons of Mass Destruction Capabilities and Programs

Nuclear	• No evidence of a nuclear weapons program. • Nuclear technological development remains at the research stage. • One research reactor in Damascus, under IAEA safeguards. • Ratified the NPT on 9/24/69; has not signed the CTBT.
Chemical	• Largest and most advanced CW capability in the Middle East. • Reported to have chemical warheads for Scud ballistic missiles, and chemical gravity bombs for delivery by aircraft. • Estimated CW stockpile in hundreds of tons. • Agents believed to include Sarin, VX, and mustard gas. • Major production facilities near Damascus and Homs, with hundreds of tons of agents produced annually. • Program remains dependent on foreign chemicals and equipment. • Not a signatory of the Chemical Weapons Convention.
Biological	• Weapons research program, but no evidence of production capability. • Signed the BTWC on 4/14/72, but has not ratified the convention.
Ballistic Missiles	• 60-120 Scud-C with 500km range and 500kg payload. • Up to 200 Scud-B missiles with 300km range and 985kg payload. • 200 SS-21 Scarab with 70km range and 480kg payload. • Developing indigenous production capability for accurate M-9 [CSS-6 or DF-15] missiles with 600km range and 500kg payload.
Cruise Missiles	• SS-N-3b Sepal with 450km range and 1,000kg payload. • SS-N-2c Styx with 80km range and 513kg payload. • Tupolev, Tu-243 unmanned aerial vehicle (UAV) with 360km range and unknown payload. • Malachite UAV with 120km range and 130kg payload.
Other Delivery Systems	• Fighter and ground-attack aircraft include: 20 Su-24; 90 Su-22; 20 MiG-29; 30 MiG-25; 44 MiG-23BN; 90 MiG-23; and 160 MiG-21. • Ground systems include field artillery and rocket launchers, notably 90+ FROG-7 artillery rockets with 18+ launchers, which have a 70km range and a 435kg payload.

Chapter 2

Recent Military Developments
in the Persian Gulf

Anthony H. Cordesman

The military balance in the Persian Gulf has changed fundamentally since the Gulf War, and the most striking of these
changes has occurred in the Northern Gulf. When Iraq in -
vaded Kuwait, it was the dominant regional military power in
the Gulf. It had decisively defeated Iran during the spring and
summer of 1988, in battles which cost Iran some 45–55 per -
cent of its inventory of major land force weapons. Further -
more, the United States and Britain had inflicted major losses
on the Iranian navy in the "tanker war" of 1987–88. Iraq had
the only modern, combat-effective armored and mechanized
forces in the Gulf and an air force that was emerging as
combat effective for the first time. It had massive missile
forces and chemical warfare capabilities, was beginning to
deploy large numbers of biological weapons, and was making
substantial progress in developing a nuclear capability.

Iraq has rebuilt and reorganized its forces that survived the
Gulf War, but now has only about one-half the land and air
capability it had when the air campaign began. It has not had
any significant imports of arms or military technology since
the summer of 1990, and has had no real opportunity to react
to many of the lessons of the Gulf War. Most of its missile,
chemical, biological, and nuclear capabilities have been dis -
mantled by United Nations Special Committee (UNSCOM) and
the International Atomic Energy Agency (IAEA), and its efforts
to develop its military industries have been severely limited by
the impact of seven years of United Nations (UN) sanctions.
Iraq's regime has not changed and it remains a significant
threat to all its neighbors. It is likely to be a revanchist state
as long as Saddam Hussein is in power and will seek to
rebuild its military power as soon as it can.

Iran in contrast, has partially recovered from its defeat in
the Iran-Iraq War and is again a major military power by Gulf
standards. It is scarcely a modern military power by the

29

standards of the United States. Many of its post-Gulf War imports have done little more than offset the steadily greater obsolescence of its Western-supplied equipment, and it has had only limited imports of modern aircraft and armor. Iran has, however, developed carefully focused military capabili - ties. The massive infantry-artillery dominated forces of the Iran-Iraq War are being replaced by forces that focus on spe - cific missions. It has developed a substantial capability to threaten shipping through the Straits of Hormuz and the rest of the Gulf, and it has developed a capability for unconven - tional warfare that it can project into the Gulf and throughout the region. It has increased steadily its missile, chemical, bio - logical warfare capabilities and is seeking nuclear weapons.

Unlike Iraq, however, Iran is in the middle of considerable political change. The election of President Mohammed Khatami in May 1997 has revealed a major split between Iran's moderate and traditional extremists. Iran has given its economy a higher priority than arms and has steadily im - proved its relations with its Southern Gulf neighbors. There is at least some prospect that the United States and Iran can reestablish diplomatic relations over the next few years, al - though no one can predict the future course of the Iranian revolution and how moderate Iran will really become.

In contrast, the Southern Gulf forces have tended to main - tain the status quo. For all the rhetoric surrounding the Gulf Cooperation Council (GCC), the Southern Gulf states remain as divided as at the start of the Gulf War. Their arms pur - chases reflect the same lack of effective standardization, in ter-operability, and focus on key missions. Some countries have made significant improvements in individual aspects of their military capabilities, but Southern Gulf military planning re - mains dominated by politics and petty rivalry, and far too many arms purchases focus on new technology and the "glit - ter factor" rather than effective war-fighting capability. Far too little real progress per dollar has been made in the effective defense of Kuwait and the Saudi border with Iraq and in dealing with mine warfare and the Iranian naval threat in the lower Gulf. Far too little emphasis has been placed on training and sustainability, and many of the arms purchases madesince the Gulf War have done little to improve military effectiveness.

There are four other major changes in the military balance that seem likely to affect the Gulf well into the twenty-first century. The Gulf states have made little progress since the Gulf War in dealing with their structural economic problems and political divisions. Iraq, whose economy had largely col - lapsed during the Iran-Iraq War, experienced a full collapse in 1991. Its Sunni, Shi'ite, and Kurdish factions are held to - gether by one of the most repressive regimes since Nazi Ger - many. Iran's per capita income has fallen to the levels Iran had in the mid-1970s, and it is unclear what Iran's long-term prospects for development will be. The Southern Gulf has talked reform but has failed to act, and its rapid population growth has cut per capita incomes far below the days of the oil boom. Ethnic, political, and economic problems have already helped lead to extremism and violence in Bahrain and Saudi Arabia. If the Gulf states finally act on their promises of reform, there is no reason to assume their current problems will lead to significant civil unrest and violence. If they do not, internal civil conflict may often be as serious a threat as Iran and Iraq.

The Gulf War has triggered a race in tactical technology , based in part on lessons drawn from the rapid US dominance of Iraq and the revolution in military affairs. It is a race, however, that lacks consistency and cohesion. UN sanctions have limited Iraq's ability to purchase new weapons and ad - vanced technology, and Iran has faced major constraints in terms of resources and access to imports of advanced weap - ons. The Southern Gulf has focused on buying individual weapons with a high "glitter factor," without proper regard for training, sustainability, maneuver capability, and joint war - fare. It has stressed the national competition for the most prestigious arms over any aspect of interoperability. Neverthe- less, some Gulf forces are beginning to focus on the revolution in military affairs and on acquiring mission-oriented packages of advanced technology rather than on building up force num- bers to the degree emphasized in the past.

The Gulf War has left a heritage of Southern Gulf depend- ence on US power projection capabilities . This dependence is reflected in strengthened United States prepositioning, in im - proved deployment facilities, and in a series of bilateral and multilateral training and exercise efforts that are far more ad-

vanced than those carried out as part of the GCC. This de -
pendence, however, creates growing doubts within the South -
ern Gulf states as to the cost-effectiveness of national defense
efforts and arms purchases. It makes the United States a
natural target for dissidents and extremists, and has the critical weakness that the United States has not been able to
preposition land equipment in Saudi Arabia—the most urgent
area in terms of Southern Gulf vulnerability.

The Gulf War and dual containment have slowed the missile
race and efforts to acquire weapons of mass destruction
(WMD). Instead, the Gulf seems locked into a process of creeping proliferation in which Iraq attempts to preserve the rem -
nants of its prewar capabilities, carry out new covert pro   -
grams, and develop a break out capability for the time when
UN sanctions are lifted. Iran, in contrast, is actively pursuing
the development and/or deployment of long-range missiles. It
is deploying chemical weapons and is carrying out covert bio -
logical and nuclear weapons programs, but at a slow and
steady pace of development rather than in the grandiose manner that Iraq pursued before the Gulf War. No Southern Gulf
state has followed up Saudi Arabia's purchase of obsolete
long-range missiles from China or shown signs of developing
WMD. Several countries are, however, beginning to explore
theater missile defense and civil defense options. The United
States increasingly focuses on counterproliferation, and the
creeping proliferation in the Gulf inevitably interacts with proliferation in the India-Pakistan arms race, the Arab-Israeli
arms race, and the search to find a counterbalance to the
conventional technology of the United States.

The arms race in the Gulf owes its origins to the cold war,
Nasserism, the fall of the Hashemite dynasty in Iraq, the Arab-
Israeli War, British withdrawal from the Gulf, the Iran-Iraq
War, and the Gulf War, and a host of minor regional quarrels.
It is also an arms race that shows no signs of ending. It is far
from clear that the Gulf is headed for war. At present, US
strength and Iranian and Iraqi weakness ensure a relatively
stable balance of deterrence in the Gulf that offsets the lack of
effective military cooperation between the Gulf states. The Gulf
remains a much less threatening place than it was dur ing the

32

worst days of the Iran-Iraq War or at the time the fighting began in 1991.

At the same time, there is no guarantee for the future. New arms purchases ensure a steady flow of new arms and tech - nology. Iran and Iraq retain major war-fighting capabilities, and the problem of proliferation not only can reshape the military balance but introduce new forms of terrorism. The Southern Gulf states have done little to create effective deter - rent and defense capabilities and have pursued their national glitter factor over regional cooperation. Creeping or not, the problem of proliferation has already arrived.

The Impact of Arms Transfers since the Gulf War

The flow of arms to the Gulf has scarcely ended. However, the end of the Iran-Iraq War, the Gulf War, UN sanctions against Iraq, and dual containment have had a major impact on the nature of military expenditures and arms imports. Iraq has lost the ability to recapitalize its military forces, much less modernize them effectively.

Iran is spending far less on both its total military forces and arms than during the Iran-Iraq War. Contrary to conventional wisdom, Southern Gulf military expenditures and arms trans- fers have also dropped significantly. At the same time, the Gulf tendency to buy a "dog's breakfast" of different arms from different sources has not changed.

Iranian military expenditures have dropped to about one- third of their Iran-Iraq War level, as measured in constant dollars. Iranian arms imports have dropped to about one-fifth to one-fourth of their Iran-Iraq War level as measured in con stant dollars. Iraqi military expenditures have dropped to about one-tenth of their Iran-Iraq War level, as measured in constant dollars. Iraq has had no major arms imports since 1990.

Southern Gulf military expenditures are now at somewhat lower levels than their average before the Gulf War. Southern Gulf arms imports now average about half of their pre-Gulf War level in constant dollars. These purchases are now driven largely by the purchases of Kuwait and the United Arab Emir - ates (UAE).

The data on deliveries of arms show that the momentum of Iran's orders during the Iran-Iraq War and during the immedi-ate crisis following its defeat in 1988 have led to sustained deliveries at higher rates than new orders. At the same time, the extraordinary volume of deliveries to Iraq before the Gulf War—some $16.6 billion worth of deliveries during 1987–90—helps explain why it has been able to sustain its reduced military force posture in spite of a cut-off of arms imports since 1990.

The data for the Southern Gulf reflect the fact that Saudi Arabia is the region's largest arms buyer. At the same time, they reflect the fact that Saudi Arabia's economic and budget deficit problems led to significant cuts in the rate of new arms orders in spite of the Gulf War. Saudi new arms agreements dropped from $45.7 billion during 1987–90 to $30.2 billion in 1991–94, and $14.1 billion in 1994–97. Once again, the scale of these cuts in Saudi new orders has often been disguised in media reporting by the momentum of deliveries from past orders. Saudi arms deliveries totaled $26.3 billion during 1987–90 and 27.9 billion in 1991–94, and then leaped to $36.4 billion in 1994–97 as deliveries caught up with the backlog of past orders. Similar trends affected Kuwait, which ordered $5.0 billion worth of arms during 1990–93 and only $2.3 billion during 1994–97, but which saw its deliveries rise from $2.4 billion in 1990–93 to $4.5 billion in 1994–97. Bah - rain and Qatar also followed in Kuwait's pattern, although the UAE has emerged a major sustained buyer. It ordered $5.3 billion worth of arms during 1990–93, and $5.1 billion during 1994–97. The UAE took delivery on $2.6 billion worth of arms in 1990–93 and $2.4 billion in 1994–97.

It is impossible to discuss all of the qualitative problems accompanying the arms purchases being made in the Gulf. It is all too clear, however, far too many Southern Gulf countries buy arms without a consistent strategy, proper regard for coa-lition warfare, or meaningful mission priorities. A review of the land force buys since 1991 reveals far too many types of differ-ent weapons from different countries. If one looks through both the naval order of battle in the Gulf and the performance characteristics of the ships purchased since 1991, many naval purchases seem to reflect a contest as to which country can buy the most complex frigate or corvette.

The problems in air orders of battle and land-based air defenses are less obvious, but there are far too many types of aircraft and short-ranged air defense systems that are not integrated into a common and fully computerized Southern Gulf-wide system or concept of air operations. Only Saudi Arabia has fully integrated airborne sensor and battle man - agement systems into its concept of air operations. Purchases for offensive air operations reflect a lack of meaningful recon - naissance and targeting capabilities, a failure to integrate bat- tle damage assessment into the loop, and a lack of integrated concepts of joint warfare.

This is not to say that individual countries have not made major progress in some areas. Nevertheless, one does not have to be a military expert to realize that buying radically different mixes of equipment from a wide range of suppliers presents major problems in terms of interoperability and standardization.

It is not coincidental that the last two US Central Command (USCENTCOM) annual seminars dealing with security assis - tance have focused on the need to provide for adequate train - ing, infrastructure, and sustainability and have stressed the fact that Southern Gulf states are buying too many major weapons. The issue is not "buy American," since Europe and Russia are perfectly capable of supplying excellent systems, many of which are better suited to Gulf needs than US sys - tems designed for long range and global deployment. The Southern Gulf states should not cease modernization or seek an edge over Iran and Iraq. They should buy wisely and at the proper rate.

Unfortunately, the cuts in oil export revenues and growing budget deficits make this even more unlikely than in the past, and there is no unifying threat serious enough to catalyze collective action. Furthermore, each Gulf state still has a large backlog of undelivered arms orders which were placed with limited regard to mission priorities, interoperability, and col - lective defense. This backlog ensures that many problems will get worse over the next few years.

For all the criticism of UN sanctions and dual containment, it is clear that they have not been without their benefits. Iraq has had virtually no arms imports since 1990. Even before the Gulf War, it would have taken about $1.5 billion a year of imports to sustain Iraq's military machine. Iraq's massive equipment losses during the Gulf War have reduced its need for imports to sustain existing systems, but have created a massive new set of requirements to rebuild Iraq's forces and act on the lessons of the Gulf War.

While it is impossible to make reliable estimates, it is diffi - cult to see how Iraq could recapitalize and modernize its forces for less than $35 to $50 billion dollars, and even if all sanctions stopped today, it would take at least one-half a decade for Iraq to buy and receive deliveries on such orders. In the interim, Iraq has no choice other than to smuggle what it can, seek to transform its military industries from centers of vainglorious rhetoric to centers of actual production, and ob - tain what it can.

Iran, on the other hand, has encountered fewer constraints. The United States and its allies have blocked many transfers of advanced arms to Iran, particularly from Europe and the former Soviet Union (FSU). Iran's revolutionary economy is also still more "revolting" than "pragmatic," and Iran's mis - management of its budget, development, and foreign debt have interacted synergistically with containment.

According to declassified US intelligence estimates, Iran signed new agreements worth $10.2 billion during the four-year period between 1987–90—the time between the final years of the Iran-Iraq War and the Gulf War. Iran's new arms agreements again dropped sharply during the four year period following the Gulf War, and totaled only $4.8 billion during 1991–94. Despite some reports of massive Iranian military build-ups—new agreements during 1991–94 totaled only a quarter of the value of the agreements that Iran had signed during the previous four years.

Iran signed only $1.6 billion worth of new arms agreements during 1994–97—a period heavily influenced by an economic crisis inside Iran, low oil revenues, and problems in repaying foreign debt. Iran ordered $200 million from Russia, $900 million from China, $100 million with other European states (mostly Eastern Europe), and $300 million from other coun - tries (mostly North Korea). The drop in agreements with Rus -

sia reflected both Iran's financial problems and the result of US pressure that had led President Boris Yeltsin not to make major new arms sales to Iran. Iran's new agreements with China and North Korea heavily emphasized missiles and mis - sile production technology. Similar trends took place in deliv - eries. Iran took delivery on $7.8 billion worth of arms in 1987–90, $3.0 billion in 1990–93, and $1.9 billion in 1994–97.

Iran's focus on WMD and systems that can threaten tanker traffic and the Southern Gulf makes Iran dangerous in spite of its relatively low level of arms imports and the obsolescence or low quality of much of its order of battle. Iran has bought enough arms to rebuild its army to the point where it can defend effectively against a weakened Iraq. It has begun to rebuild its air force and land-based air defenses and can put up a far more effective defense than in 1988. It has restruc - tured its regular forces and the Iranian Revolutionary Guard Corps (IRGS) to improve the defense of its Southern Gulf coast and create a far more effective ability to attack naval forces, tanker traffic, offshore facilities, and targets along the South - ern Gulf coast.

Conventional Threats from Iran and Iraq

There is no way to summarize the threats Iran and Iraq can pose in the Gulf without resorting to military shorthand and without talking about capabilities rather than intentions. There is no way to predict the future behavior of either regime, or to discuss the nuances of its present and near-term mili - tary capabilities. It is also important to reiterate the fact that a combination of United States, British, and Southern Gulf mili- tary forces is presently capable of defeating virtually any con - ventional war-fighting threat from either state if it acts with sufficient speed, unity, and determination.

The only near-term developments that could alter this bal - ance would be (1) a major cutback in US power projection capability or Southern Gulf support, (2) the institutionaliza - tion of a significant low level internal conflict in a Southern Gulf state that Iran or Iraq could exploit and which would confront the United States with the fact that it cannot save a Gulf government from its own people, or (3) the sudden transfer of a nuclear weapon or sufficient fissile material for   a "break out" in building a bomb—a development that could radically change United States and Southern Gulf perceptions of the risk in taking military action.

The Threat from Iran

It is easy to talk about Iran as seeking to be a hegemon or trying to dominate the Gulf, but it is unclear what this really means. Iran has a regime that is hostile to the West and its neighbors in many ways, but this hostility does not translate into a predictable willingness to start a conflict. Iran's revolu - tionary rhetoric is mixed with statements describing its good intentions, and threats are mixed with defensiveness. Iran faces powerful limits to its ability to import arms, develop its weapons of mass destruction, and create effective military forces. It has to deal with the fact that every hostile or threat- ening act it takes is likely to provoke a reaction from the United States, Southern Gulf states, and Iraq.

Focusing on major Iranian military buildups, and Iran's capability to fight a large regional war does little to explain the complex trends in Iran's military forces. In fact, such efforts are likely to do more to disguise the range of issues and possibilities that need to be analyzed than provide a meaning- ful way of summarizing Iran's military capabilities. At the same time, Iran's military future is not an exercise in chaos theory. The previous analysis has shown that many broad trends in its military behavior and capabilities are highly pre- dictable, at least in the near term. While it is impossible to dismiss a long list of wild card events and changes, it is possible to summarize the most probable trends in Iran's mili- tary future by looking at a range of the most likely contingen - cies and Iran's present and future capabilities.

Iran cannot win a naval-air battle against US forces in the Gulf and has no prospect of doing so in the foreseeable future. It would have to rebuild and modernize both its regular navy and air force at levels of strength and capability it simply cannot hope to achieve in the next decade. Alternatively, it would need to develop its capabilities to deliver WMD to the point where it could back its conventional military capabilities with a threat that might seriously inhibit US military action and/or the willingness of Southern Gulf states to support the United States and provide air and naval facilities.

The wild cards in such contingencies are the US determina-tion to act, the size of the United States presence in the Gulf and US power projection capabilities at the time of a given crisis, Southern Gulf support for the United States, and will -ingness to provide the United States with suitable facilities, and the political liabilities the United States would face in terms of the response from nations outside the region. Far more is involved in a confrontation in the Gulf than military capability, and Iran would have far more contingency capabil-ity if the United States could not respond for political or budg-etary reasons.

Iran has a rough overall military parity with Iraq, although it could not sustain a massive land offensive against Iraq's mili-tary forces. Iran has long had the naval and air capabilities to defeat Iraq's negligible naval strength and deny Iraq naval and commercial access to the Gulf. Iran is slowly increasing the capabilities of its land and air forces relative to those of Iraq, and its ability to use chemical warfare in another Iran-Iraq conflict. Iran is now a much stronger defensive power than in 1988, both because of Iran's force improvements and because of Iraq's defeat and the sanctions that have followed.

Iran and Iraq also steadily improved their relations during 1997 and 1998, exchanging prisoners of war, establishing trade relations, and opening their borders. Large numbers of Iranian religious pilgrims entered Iran for the first time in nearly two decades in 1998. This improvement in relations is a matter of expediency, rather than friendship, but it has eased the risk of accidental conflicts and has eased military tensions between the two countries.

Iran has steadily improved its relations with its Southern Gulf neighbors, particularly Saudi Arabia, since the election of President Khatami. It seems to be pursuing a more moderate political course towards all the Southern Gulf states. Further-more, there is little present prospect that Iran will develop enough power projection capability and supporting power from its navy, air force, and weapons of mass destruction to win any conflict in the Southern Gulf, or to force its way in sup port of a coup or uprising. This contingency is also the one most likely to unite the United States and the Southern Gulf states and to ensure European and other support for a strong US-Southern Gulf response.

At the same time, there are wild cards affecting Iranian military involvement in the Southern Gulf. Iran might seek to exploit the fracture lines and political unrest within and be - tween the Southern Gulf states. This is particularly true of the Shi'ite in Bahrain and Saudi Arabia, but it might also prove true of future confrontations between Bahrain and Qatar and Saudi Arabia and Yemen.

The United States would face serious problems in respond - ing to any change of government in a Southern Gulf state that resulted in a pro-Iranian regime and which sought Iranian military advice or an Iranian military presence. The United States cannot save a Gulf regime from its own people or openly endorse such action by other Southern Gulf countries.

Iran's process of creeping proliferation is making enough progress so that the United States and the Southern Gulf states must reach agreement on taking suitable counterproliferation measures. A power vacuum in which Iran proliferates, the Southern Gulf states grow steadily more vulnerable, and United States resolve seems progressively more questionable could give Iran far more capability to directly or indirectly intervene in Southern Gulf affairs.

Iran has already demonstrated that it is steadily improving its ability to conduct "proxy wars" by training, arming, and funding movements like the Hezbollah. IRGC and the Quds Force are likely to continue to exploit such methods as long as they are directed to do so by the Iranian regime, and there is little that can be done to force Iran to stop.

At the same time, Iran's confrontation with Afghanistan pits a Shi'ite religious regime against a much more extreme Tali - ban regime in Afghanistan. Iran has increasingly supplied arms and aid to the opposition to the Taliban, and deployed several hundred thousand troops for exercises on the Afghan border in the fall of 1998—after the Taliban massacre of Ira - nian diplomats and advisors aiding Shi'ite forces in Western Afghanistan. A major conflict between Iran and Afghanistan, or even levels of tension that forced Iran to establish a second front of major troop deployments along its border with Afghanistan would limit its ability to threaten the Gulf or Iraq.

Iran has steadily improving capabilities for unconventional warfare, including the potential use of chemical and biological weapons. The practical problem that Iran faces is finding a place and contingency where it can exploit such capabilities. The key wild cards affecting this set of contingencies are Iran's willingness to take the risk of using such forces and alienating other states, the uncertain value of such adventures to Iran, and the willingness of other states and non-Persian movements to accept such Iranian support and the probable political price tag.

The previous contingencies assume that Iran will take offensive action. If it does, it may well be confronted with a US-led attack on Iran. If this attack is confined to naval and coastal targets, particularly those Iranian military capabilities that potentially threaten Gulf shipping, there is little Iran can do other than try to ride out the attack by dispersing and hiding its smaller boats and antiship missiles.

If a US-led attack includes strategic conventional missile strikes and bombings, there is little Iran can do in immediate response other than escalate by using WMD in ways that are more likely to end in increasing the risk and damage to Iran than to deter or damage US forces. Iran can, however, respond over time with terrorism, unconventional warfare, and proxy wars. It is much easier for air and missile power to inflict major damage on Iran than it is to predict or control the political and military aftermath. The resulting casualties and damage will be extremely difficult to translate into an end game.

Attacks on the Iranian mainland that went beyond a punitive raid would be much more costly. A US-led coalition could defeat Iran's regular forces, but would have to be at least corps level in size, and occupying Iran would be impractical without massive land forces of several entire corps. Even lim ited amphibious and land attacks on the mainland would expose the invading forces to a much higher risk of low intensity and guerrilla combat with Iranian forces that constantly received reinforcement and resupply. Further, Iran's use of terrorism and WMD would be politically easier to justify in a defensive conflict than an offensive one. Such attacks would probably end in futility, and in creating a revanchist Iran.

The previous contingencies assume that Iran's strength will be determined largely by the war-fighting capabilities of its military forces. Iran may, however, be able to achieve some of its objectives through intimidation and direct and indirect threats. Iran's ability to provide such threats will improve steadily in the near to mid-term, in spite of its military weakness. In many cases, its neighbors may be willing to accommodate Iran to some degree. This is particularly true of those states whose gas and oil resources are most exposed—like Qatar—or which see Iraq as a more serious threat—like Kuwait.

Iraq's Military Future

It is unrealistic to hope for "moderation" in Saddam Hussein's regime, or to expect that a new leader will bring a complete end to Iraq's challenge to its neighbors and the West, or its efforts to proliferate. The Gulf War did not change Saddam's fundamental behavior and neither has the "war of in - spections." Saddam's most probable near-term successors are likely to be products of the Ba'ath, Saddam's coterie and/or the military rather than true moderates. They are also likely to be minority Sunnis from some mix of clans and tribes rather than a true national government. While no one can rule out the possibility of an Iraqi Ataturk or Sadat, such leadership is more likely to change Iraq's image, and moderate the more controversial aspects of its behavior, rather than change its fundamental strategic perspective.

Iraq's mid- to long-term prospects are more favorable. It is unlikely that any sequence of ruling elites will continue to ignore Iraq's pressing demographic and economic problems to the extent that Saddam has, or that any successor can pro vide the same mix of political skills and reckless ambition. However, it is unclear when a true national leadership will come to power that can bridge Iraq's deep divisions by religion, ethnic group, tribe, and clan. Iraq is likely to have authoritarian minority leaders for some time to come, and Iraq's geography alone makes it likely that its rulers will believe they must compete with Iran, Saudi Arabia, and the United States for regional influence and power. Iraq is not proliferating simply because its current regime is radical and extreme, it is prolif   erating because it has good and enduring strategic reasons to do so.

The West and other Gulf states need to accept this reality. They need to understand the fact that they have a vital inter - est in maintaining export controls on weapons and dual-use items and in the efforts of UNSCOM and the IAEA, just as long as such controls and efforts can be maintained. They need to understand that arms control negotiations with Iraq will be an extension of the war of inspections by other means, and that only strong military forces and counterproliferation efforts can deter and defend against Iraq's break-out capabilities and a post-sanctions expansion of its proliferation effort. The world has to learn to live with the true nature of Iraq's strategic culture and its unpredictability and opportunism.

At the same time, some of Iraq's near-term contingency capabilities are predictable. While it is impossible to dismiss a long list of wild card events and changes, it is possible to summarize the most probable trends in Iraq's military future by looking at a range of the most likely contingencies and Iraq's present and future capabilities in each such contingency.

Iraq's land forces still retain significant war-fighting capa - bilities and much of the force structure that made Iraq the dominant military power in the Gulf after its victory over Iran. Iraqi forces can still seize Kuwait in a matter of days or occupy part of Saudi Arabia's Eastern Province if they do not face immediate opposition from the United States, Kuwaiti, and Saudi forces. USCENTCOM and other US experts indicate that Iraq could assemble and deploy five heavy divisions south into Kuwait in a matter of days. Iraqi divisions now have an authorized strength of about 10,000 men, and about one-half of the Iraqi army's 23 divisions had manning levels of around eight thousand men and a fair state of readiness. Republican Guard divisions had an average of around 8,000 to 10,000 men. Brigades averaged around 2,500 men—the size of a large US battalion.

Even today, Iraq has five Republican Guard divisions within 140 kilometers of the Kuwaiti and Saudi border. It can rapidly deploy two to five divisions against Kuwait from the area around Basra. A recent background briefing by USCENTCOM indicates that Kuwait could only rapidly deploy a few combat strength battalions to defend its territory, and Saudi Arabia would take days to deploy even one heavy brigade into areas north of Kuwait City. The tyranny of geography, Kuwait's small size, and Saudi Arabia's widely dispersed army give Iraq a natural advantage in any sudden or surprise attack.

The failure of Kuwait and Saudi Arabia to develop any meaningful cooperative defense plans compounds the problem, as does Saudi Arabia's miserable performance in modernizing its land forces. While Saudi Arabia and Kuwait have developed relatively effective air forces at the squadron level, they cannot fight as integrated air forces without massive US assistance and would still face major problems in coalition warfare.

The land balance is dismal. Kuwait dreamed of a 12-brigade force after the Gulf War, but it has only two understrength active brigades and two reserve brigades. Its land forces total only 11,000 personnel, and this total includes 1,600 foreign contract personnel, most of whom are noncombatants. The total manpower of the Kuwaiti armed forces, including the air force and navy, total about one US brigade (combat manpower plus support). The Kuwaiti army has an active tank strength of only about 75 M-84s (Yugoslav T-72s) and 174 M-1A2s. It is experiencing major problems in converting to the M-1A2 and has been forced to store 75 of its M-84s plus another 17 Chieftains.

Saudi Arabia is choking on massive deliveries of arms, and its army has reverted to a static defensive force with limited effectiveness above the company and battalion level. Although it claims to have 70,000 fulltime regulars in the army, plus 57,000 active members of the national guard, actual manning levels are significantly lower. About 200 of its M-1A2 tanks are in storage, plus about 145 of its 295 AMX-30s. As a result, Saudi Arabia relies heavily on its 450 M-60A3s. This is still a significant amount of armor, but it is dispersed over much of the kingdom, and Saudi Arabia lacks the training, manpower quality, sustainability, and command, control, communications, computers, and intelligence (C^{4}I)/SR capabilities for effective aggressive maneuver warfare and forward defense. While there are reports of a GCC rapid reaction force, the reality is a few hollow allied battalions. The GCC is a military myth.

Unless there are weeks of strategic warning, Kuwait, Saudi Arabia, and the United States will lack the land forces to stop Iraq. A force of five Iraqi divisions would compare favorably with total Kuwaiti forces of about four brigades, with only about a brigade equivalent combat ready, and with a total forward-deployed US strength that normally does not include a single forward-deployed land brigade. The Saudi forces at Hafr al Batin are at most the equivalent of two combat-effec - tive brigades which would probably take two weeks to fully deploy forward to the Kuwait and Saudi borders in sustain - able, combat-ready form. The so-called GCC rapid deployment force is largely a political fiction with no meaningful real-world combat capability against Iraqi heavy divisions.

There is little prospect that this situation will improve in the near term. The United States has not been able to preposition large numbers of equipment sets in or near Kuwait, and pre - positioning brigade sets in Qatar and the UAE means that such forces would take at least a week to 10 days to deploy in combat-ready form in Kuwait. Kuwait is making only limited progress in its military modernization, and the Saudi Army has made little progress in improving its capability to move quickly to the defense of Kuwait or to concentrate its forces along the Saudi border with Iraq.

As a result, the ability to deal with a sudden Iraqi attack on Kuwait is likely to depend on US ability to mass offensive air and missile power and use it immediately against Iraq the moment major troop movements begin without first seeking to win air superiority or air supremacy. The United States will also require the full support of Saudi Arabia and the other Southern Gulf countries to assist in the deployment and bas - ing of US forces in the region, support from friendly local forces like the Saudi Air Force, and a firm and immediate Kuwaiti willingness to allow the United States and Saudi Ara - bia to employ force.

Even then, the defense of Kuwait will be an increasingly close run thing. Even today, if Iraq was willing to take very high losses, Iraqi land forces might penetrate Kuwait City in spite of the United States, Saudi, and Kuwaiti airpower. If Iraq then took the Kuwaiti population hostage, it might succeed. The only way that Iraqi forces could then be dislodged would be

45

through a combination of another land build up in Saudi Arabia by the United States and allied forces, and a massive stra te-gic/ interdiction air campaign against targets on Iraqi territory.

The essential dilemma in any second liberation of Kuwait would be United States, Saudi, and Kuwaiti willingness to act in the face of potential massacres of Kuwaiti civilians, versus the willingness of an Iraqi regime to accept massive damage to Iraq. It seems likely that the United States and Saudi Arabia would show the necessary ruthlessness if the Kuwaiti govern - ment supported such action. Oil is too strategically important to cede such a victory to a leader like Saddam Hussein.

The outcome might be different, however, as sanctions ease or end, and Iraq rebuilds more of its military capabilities. There are a number of wild cards in such a case. Iraq may somehow obtain nuclear weapons, or demonstrate the posses-sion of highly lethal biological weapons. The United States may be forced to reduce its forward presence and readiness in the Gulf to the point where it could not rapidly surge air - power, and/or had to reduce its overall power projection capa-bilities. Iraq may choose a more limited objective like restoring its pre-Gulf War border or demanding access to Bubiyan, Warbah, the Kwar Abdullah, and the Gulf. Saudi Arabia may not immediately fully support US action and commit its own forces. The Kuwaiti government may refuse to accept the cost of continuing to fight in the face of ruthless Iraqi action against a hostage Kuwaiti people.

Civil War in Iraq

Iraq's forces have already shown that they have the military strength to defeat that country's lightly armed Kurds in a mat-ter of weeks if UN forces cease to protect them. The Iraqi army has effectively defeated all serious Shi'ite resistance. It would take a massive uprising, and possibly a major division within Iraq's military forces, for any civil conflict to challenge the regime.

Power is now so centralized among Sunni tribal elites , who control virtually all senior posts in the military and security forces, that any struggle for power seems more likely to take the form of a coup and counter-coup than civil war. Neverthe-less, no one can dismiss the possibility that Saddam Hussein will take another major military risk and end in making an - other strategic mistake. Saddam may well be able to survive the present situation, but not another major defeat.

It is possible that the Iraqi military could split over the struggle for power after Saddam, and combine warlordism with regional and ethnic alliances. Any serious north-south split within the army could trigger a significant civil conflict, although it is impossible to predict the resulting balance of power and ethnic and political alignments. Such a struggle might also trigger limited Iranian and Turkish intervention.

Confrontation in the Gulf

Iraq has almost none of the assets necessary to win a naval-air battle against US forces in the Gulf, and has no prospect of acquiring these assets in the foreseeable future. It would have to rebuild, modernize, and massively expand both its regular navy and air force at levels of strength and capability it simply cannot hope to achieve for the next half-decade. Alternatively, Iraq could develop its capabilities to deliver weapons of mass destruction to the point where it could back its conventional military capabilities with a threat that might seriously inhibit US military action and/or the willingness of Southern Gulf states to support the United States and provide air and naval facilities.

Unlike Iran, Iraq cannot conduct meaningful surface ship, naval air force, and amphibious operations. Currently, the Iraqi navy can only conduct limited mine warfare, land-based antiship missile attacks, and surprise raids on off-shore facilities. Its air force may be able to conduct limited antiship missile attacks using its Mirage F-1s, but would have to find a permissive environment to survive. Iraqi Mirage F-1s, bur - dened with the AM-39 Exocet, would be unlikely to survive Kuwaiti, Saudi, or Iranian air defenses without a level of air escort capability that Iraq cannot currently provide.

Iraq has little ability to intimidate its neighbors into accept - ing such operations as long as the United States has the ability to use its air and missile power to inflict enough strategic damage on Iraq to create a massive deterrent to any Iraqi escalation to chemical or biological weapons, and back these capabilities with the ultimate threat of US theater nuclear escalation. This does not mean that Iraqi air and/or naval forces could not score some gains from a sudden, well-planned raid in the Gulf. Iraq could not sustain any initial success, however, and would probably accomplish nothing more than provoke a United States, Southern Gulf, or Iranian reaction that would far offset any advantages Iraq could gain. The only exception might be a proxy unconventional or terrorist attack that al - lowed Iraq to preserve some degree of plausible deniability.

The wild cards in such contingencies are US determination to act, the future size of the US presence in the Gulf, US ability to surge its power projection capabilities at the time of a given crisis, Southern Gulf support for the United States and willingness to provide the United States with suitable facilities, and the political liabilities the United States would face in terms of the response from nations outside the region. Far more is involved in a confrontation in the Gulf than Iraq's military capability, and Iraq will be able to acquire far more contingency capability if the United States could not respond for political or budgetary reasons.

Similarly, much will depend over time on Iranian, Southern Gulf, and Western reactions to Iraq's efforts to rebuild the naval strike capability of its air force and to build up a mean - ingful blue water navy. A passive response would obviously strengthen Iraq. So would any indifference to Iraqi efforts to improve its access to the Gulf by renewing its pressure on Kuwait to grant Iraq access to Bubiyan and Warbah, or to secure the channels to Umm Qasr. Even then, however, it is difficult to see how Iraq can acquire much contingency capa - bility beyond the upper Gulf, unless Iran and/or Saudi Arabia are indifferent or supportive of Iraqi action.

Confrontation or Conflict with Iran

Iranian and Iraqi relations are improving, and both coun - tries currently seem committed to avoiding another round of fighting. There also are good military reasons for both coun - tries to avoid such a conflict. The cumulative impact of UN sanctions is slowly eroding the capabilities of Iraqi land and air forces relative to those of Iran, and Iraq has only limited ability to use chemical warfare in another Iran-Iraq conflict.

Iraq cannot hope to challenge Iran's naval strength or deny Iran naval and commercial access to the Gulf. Iran is now a much stronger defensive power than it was in 1988, both because of Iran's force improvements and because of Iraq's defeat and the sanctions that have followed.

It is far from clear, however, that Iran will acquire enough of an edge over Iraq to win a major conflict and avoid a repetition of the grinding war of attrition that took place during the Iran-Iraq War. In spite of Saddam Hussein, the Iraqi army seems more likely to unite in a defensive conflict than to divide, and it still has nearly twice Iran's tank strength and a superior air force.

The wild cards in any contingencies involving a conflict be-tween Iran and Iraq are the possibility of internal unrest and divisions in Iraq that are serious enough to split the Iraqi armed forces, and/or which lead to a new Shi'ite uprising. Similarly, a major Kurdish uprising would greatly complicate Iraq's ability to concentrate its forces to defend against an Iranian attack on Iraq's center and south.

If such a contingency does occur, any Iranian victory over Iraq might prove to be more apparent than real. It is far from clear that the United States or Southern Gulf states would tolerate an Iranian victory that did more than depose the present Iraqi regime. Further, the split between Persian, Arab, and Kurd seems likely to remain so great that Iraqi inde-pendence would rapidly reassert itself if Iran attempted to occupy or dominate a substantial part of Iraq.

Further, an escalation to the use of weapons of mass de-struction against urban, economic, and large military area targets could introduce great uncertainties into such a con-flict. Iran now has a major advantage in terms of biological and chemical weapons and this advantage will grow steadily until UN sanctions on Iraq are lifted. Iraq could then rebuild its strategic delivery capabilities relatively quickly, however, and the end result of any sustained conflict of this kind would be difficult to predict.

The greatest single uncertainty would be the development and use of advanced biological weapons with near nuclear lethality or the assembly and use of a nuclear device assem-bled with weapons grade fissile material bought from an out-

side source. There may be little or no warning of such   a
strategic development, and the United States is unlikely to
extend its deterrent coverage over either Iran or Iraq. Another
wild card is that a United States or Israeli counterproliferation
strike on either Iraq or Iran could make the target vulnerable
enough for the other country to exploit the resulting window
of opportunity.

Adventures in the Southern Gulf

There is little near-term prospect that Iraq   will develop
enough power projection capability and supporting power
from its navy, air force, and WMD to win any conflict in the
Southern Gulf where it does not attack by land into Kuwait or
across the Saudi border. The only exception would seem to be
a case where it operated in support of a coup or uprising, or
when Iraqi volunteers operated in Southern Yemen in 1994.
Any Iraqi attack on a Southern Gulf state is also the contin -
gency most likely to unite the United States and the Southern
Gulf states and to ensure European and other support for a
strong US-Southern Gulf response.

At the same time, there are three important wild cards af -
fecting Iraqi military involvement in the Southern Gulf. Noth -
ing can prevent Iraq from exploiting the fracture lines within
and between the Southern Gulf states. Iraq has much less
capacity than Iran to exploit the Shi'ite unrest in Bahrain and
Saudi Arabia, but it might be able to exploit future confronta -
tions between Bahrain and Qatar and Saudi Arabia and
Yemen. The United States would face serious problems in   re-
sponding to any change of government in a Southern Gulf
state that resulted in a pro-Arab/pro-Iraqi regime and which
sought Iraqi military advice or an Iraqi military presence. The
United States cannot save a Gulf regime from its own people   or
openly endorse such action by other Southern Gulf countries.
Iraq's process of creeping proliferation is making enough pro -
gress so that the United States and the Southern Gulf states
must reach some degree of agreement on taking suitable
counterproliferation measures. A power vacuum in which Iraq
proliferates, the Southern Gulf states grow steadily more vul -
nerable, and US resolve seems progressively more question   -

able, could give Iraq far more capability to directly or indi -
rectly intervene in Southern Gulf affairs.

Wars Against Israel

At least in the near-term, Iraq is so weak that it seems
unlikely that it would directly provoke Israel by doing anything
more than sending limited forces to Jordan or Syria if another
major conflict should somehow take place between Israel and
its key neighbors. Iraq could move a corps size force into
Jordan or Syria within a matter of days, although it would
take weeks to give it the substantial capability needed to sustain itself in intensive combat. It could also deploy air units,
although it presently does not have the ability to operate
within the Jordanian or Syrian C ^{4}I/battle management (BM)
and identification of friend or foe (IFF) system. Improving this
situation requires the extensive rebuilding of Iraq's military
capabilities, and joint exercises with Jordan and/or Syria.

Until recently, such a prospect seemed very doubtful as
Jordan has made peace with Israel, and King Hussein actively
supported Iraqi opposition movements during 1994–96. Syria
fought against Iraq in the Gulf War, and its President Hafez
al-Assad, has long been a bitter rival of Saddam Hussein. The
deterioration of the Arab-Israel peace process in 1996–98,
however, led Syria to take a progressively harder line towards
Israel and to reach out for new allies. At the same time, Iraq's
search to end sanctions and break out of its containment led
it to approach Syria. Iraq and Syria began to hold serious
meetings for the first time in half a decade. The border was
opened for limited traffic and key Iraqi papers like *Babel* began to call for Iraqi-Syrian military cooperation, and for Iraq
and Syria to resume diplomatic ties.

It seems unlikely that any Arab-Israeli conflict would
broaden to include Egypt or Jordan, as long as President
Mohammad Hosni Mubarak, King Hussein's son, or any other
moderate leaders remain in power. Assad has shown little
interest in taking such risks and remains hostile to Saddam
Hussein. Iraq must also realize that it is extremely unlikely
that Israel will show restraint in any future missile war, and
would probably escalate to the use of nuclear weapons if Iraq

made any attributable use of weapons of mass destruction against Israel's civilian population or large formations of Is - raeli military forces.

Turkey and the Kurds

Iraq is more likely to seek a tacit or open Turkish alliance against the Kurds than to seek military confrontation. There are, however, two possibilities for conflict. One is a future Iraqi-Turkish alliance in the form of coordinated operations against the Kurds in the northern border area. Such an alli - ance would offer Turkey the prospect of denying its rebel Kurdish factions sanctuary and bases in the Iraqi border area, and offer Iraq both support in suppressing its Kurds and the prospect that Turkey would cease its raids across the border. Both nations have a strong incentive to secure the area to allow them to improve trade and the security of Iraq's pipeline through Turkey.

It is also possible, however, that Turkey's constant incur - sions into Iraq's border area could trigger some kind of low level fighting if Iraq's military forces should reoccupy the Kurdish security zone. Iraqi senior officials have increasingly protested Turkey's military actions in Iraq, and its estab - lishment of a security zone inside Iraq to halt Kurdish attacks on Turkey. Many senior Iraqi officials also seem to fear that Turkey might still attempt to annex some part of northern Iraq, including some of the oil fields in the area. These fears of Turkish ambitions are almost certainly exaggerated, but they are still very real.

Proxy Wars

Unlike Iran, Iraq has never demonstrated much capability to conduct proxy wars by training, arming, and funding Arab extremist movements. Iraq does sponsor some extremist and terrorist groups, but the end result has done little for Iraq. Iraq also lacks Iran's bases, training centers, and staging fa cili- ties in other countries, and the political support of third nations like the Sudan and Syria which are close to the scene of such proxy conflicts. Similarly, Iraq can only hope to win proxy wars fought against vulnerable governments. Attempts to fight such wars will have little impact on a successful Arab-Israeli peace settlement, or in sustaining civil conflict in the face of a government that demonstrates that it has the capacity to govern and deal with its social problems.

At the same time, the failure of the peace process and of secular regimes may make Iraq's use of proxy wars more successful in the future. So would the creation of a radical Arab regime in Jordan, Egypt, or Syria, which might turn to Iraq for support. Iraq also has a strong revanchist motive to use proxy warfare against Israel, Saudi Arabia, and the United States.

Unconventional Offensive Conflicts

Similarly, Iraq may seek to improve its capabilities for unconventional warfare, including the use of chemical and biological weapons. The practical problem that Iraq faces will be to find a place and contingency where it can exploit such capabilities that offer more return than using proxies, and which allows Iraq to act at an acceptable level of risk.

In broad terms, there do not seem to be any current contingencies where Iraq can achieve major gains by using unconventional military forces in offensive warfare. The closest case seems to be Turkey's struggle with its Kurds, but Turkey is an extraordinarily dangerous opponent for Iraq to provoke, and any Iraqi aid to Turkey's Kurds would present further problems in Iraq's efforts to control its own Kurds.

The key wild cards affecting this set of contingencies are Iraq's willingness to take the risk of using its unconventional forces and alienating other states, the uncertain value of such adventures, and the willingness of other states and movements to accept such Iraqi support and the political price tag that would come with it. This situation might change if Iraq could send volunteers to Lebanon and Syria under circumstances where such conflicts had broad Arab support, and Israel was sufficiently preoccupied with other threats so that it could not retaliate; actively supporting some opposition force in Iran appeared to be a safe way of limiting the Iranian threat or ending Iranian support for anti-Iraqi movements; supporting an alienated Yemen offered Iraq a low cost way of using unconventional forces to threaten or put pressure on Saudi

Arabia; support of some movement in Turkey seemed likely to gain Iraq broader support in Turkey; and a civil conflict took place in Kuwait or Saudi Arabia.

None of these contingencies now seem likely. At the same time, the risks of Iraq using its unconventional warfare capa - bilities should not be discounted. If nothing else, Iraq might act in a spoiler role, attempting to deny some other nation influence even if Iraq could not make clear strategic gains on its own.

The Defense of Iraq

The previous contingencies assume that Iraq will take offensive action. If it does, it may well be confronted with a US-led attack. If this attack is confined to naval and coastal targets, particularly those Iraqi military capabilities that potentially threaten Gulf shipping, there is little Iraq can do other than try to ride out the attack by dispersing and hiding its smaller boats and antiship missiles.

If a US-led attack includes strategic conventional missile strikes and bombings, there is equally little Iraq can do in terms of an immediate response, other than to escalate to using weapons of mass destruction in ways that are more likely to end in increasing the risk and damage to Iraq than to deter or damage US forces. Iraq can, however, respond over time with terrorism, unconventional warfare, and proxy wars. It is much easier to use air and missile power to inflict major damage on Iraq than it is to predict or control the political and military aftermath. The resulting casualties and damage will be extremely difficult to translate into an end game.

Any US use of amphibious and land warfare would be con - siderably more difficult. Iraq can probably mount a significant defense against amphibious attacks on its coastline and is - lands. It is impossible to dismiss a popular Shi'ite or Kurdish uprising in support of an outside attack, but the most likely response would seem to be that Iraq's population would unite or remain passive while United States or coalition forces were forced to advance over water barriers and through built-up areas.

The Iraqi army might collapse in the face of such an ass ault, but the Republican Guard is more likely to dig in and defend from positions co-located with Iraq's civil population, which would limit the ability to exploit airpower. Attacks on Iraqi territory that went beyond a punitive raid might be costly.

A US-led coalition could probably defeat Iraq's forces, but would have to be at least corps level in size, and occupying Iraq would be impractical without massive land forces of sev - eral corps. Further, Iraq's use of terrorism and weapons of mass destruction would be much easier to justify politically in a defensive conflict rather than an offensive one. Such outside attacks would probably end in futility, and in creating an even more revanchist Iraq.

As for the Iraqi opposition, its vainglorious claims to mili tary effectiveness are largely meaningless. The deeply divided Kurd - ish forces have proved to be more interested in fighting each other than Iraq, and every temporary alliance between the Barzani and Talibani factions has collapsed. The claims of the Iraqi National Congress (INC) to have set up a military force in the Kurdish Security Zone, before Iraq reentered the area in 1996 and destroyed the INC's operation, consisted of several hundred badly trained and equipped men organized into a force that would have required thousands to be effective. In spite of some US efforts to help create an opposition force, the only way the US could count on help would be if part of the regular Iraqi army defected—something that seems unlikely.

Exploiting Wars of Intimidation

The previous contingencies assume that Iraq's strength will be determined largely by the war-fighting capabilities of its military forces. Iraq may, however, be able to achieve some of its objectives through intimidation and/or direct and indirect threats. Iraq's ability to provide such intimidation is now very limited but will improve steadily once UN sanctions are lifted. In many cases, Iraq's neighbors may be willing to increasingly accommodate Iran. This is particularly true of those states like Bahrain, Oman, Qatar, and the UAE which see Iran as a serious threat.

Much will depend upon regional perceptions of the long-term resolve of the United States , the ability of the Southern Gulf states to avoid major divisions, and the willingness of the

Southern Gulf states to show they will support a firm US response to Iraq, even at some risk. Much will also depend on the ability of Iraq's leadership to set achievable demands and avoid open confrontation. In broad terms, it seems likely that Iraq's ability to intimidate will slowly improve over time, but there is no way to predict how quickly or by how much.

Iran, Iraq, and Weapons of Mass Destruction

It is possible to conduct endless debates over the serious - ness of Iran's efforts to proliferate and Iraq's potential success in retaining some of the capabilities it possessed at the time of the Gulf War, developing a covert break out capability in spite of UNSCOM and the IAEA, and rearming once sanctions are lifted.

Iran's effort to acquire chemical, biological, and nuclear weapons and suitable long-range strike systems are tools to an end, and weapons of mass destruction do not necessarily make radical changes in Iran's contingency capabilities. At the same time, such weapons give Iran a post-Gulf War edge over Iraq. They also inevitably affect US, British, Israeli, and Southern Gulf perceptions of the risks inherent in attacking Iran. Much depends upon these perceptions of the risk in engaging Iran, refusing its demands, and dealing with Iranian escalation and/or retaliation.

It seems unlikely that Iran's creeping proliferation will reach the point in the near-term where Iran's capabilities are great enough to change US, British, Israeli, and/or Southern Gulf perceptions of risk to the point where they would limit or paralyze outside military action. Further, it seems unlikely that Iran can continue to build up its capabilities without provok - ing even stronger US counterproliferation programs, including retaliatory strike capabilities. The same is true of a response from Iraq and the Southern Gulf states. As a result, Iran's creeping proliferation may end in provoking a creeping arms race. Arms races do not, however, always bring deterrence and stability. Further, four wild cards deserve special atten - tion:

- a successful Iranian attempt to buy significant amounts of weapons grade material,

- a change in the United States and regional perception of biological weapons,
- Iraq may find a way to end UN sanctions and/or reveal a substantial break-out capability of its own, and
- Iran might use such weapons through proxies or in covert attacks with some degree of plausible deniability.

Iraq's present holdings of chemical and biological weapons are so limited that they do not constrain US freedom of action, or do much to intimidate Iraq's neighbors. Also, Iran now has a significant lead over Iraq. Nevertheless, Iraq's possession of such weapons inevitably affects the United States, British, Israeli, and Southern Gulf perceptions of the risks inherent in attacking Iraq. Much depends upon these outside perceptions of the risk in engaging Iraq, in refusing its demands, and dealing with Iraqi aggression and/or retaliation.

It seems unlikely that Iraq can reach the point, in the near-term, where its capabilities are great enough to change US, British, Israeli, and/or Southern Gulf perceptions of risk to the point where they would limit or paralyze outside military action. Further, it seems unlikely that Iraq can continue to build up its capabilities without provoking strong US counter-proliferation programs, including retaliatory strike capabilities. The same is true of a response by Iran and the Southern Gulf states. As a result, Iraq's acquisition of weapons of mass de - struction may end simply in provoking an arms race even when UN sanctions are lifted.

Once again, however, arms races scarcely always end in deterrence and stability. As is the case with Iran, several wild cards deserve special attention. A successful Iraqi attempt to buy significant amounts of weapons grade material could al - low Iraq to achieve a nuclear break out capability in a matter of months. Both the United States and the region would find it much harder to adjust to such an Iraqi effort than to the slow development of nuclear weapons by creating fissile material in Iraq. It seems likely that the United States could deal with the situation by extending a nuclear umbrella over the Gulf, but even so, the Southern Gulf states might be far more respon - sive to Iraqi pressure and intimidation. Most, after all, are so small that they are virtually "one bomb states."

Biological weapons are now largely perceived as unproven systems of uncertain lethality. Regardless of their technical capabilities, they have little of the political impact of nuclear weapons. Iraq might, however, conduct live animal tests to demonstrate that its biological weapons have near-nuclear le - thality or some other power might demonstrate their effective - ness in another conflict. The successful mass testing or use of biological weapons might produce a rapid paradigm shift in the perceived importance of such weapons and of Iraq's bio - logical warfare programs.

Iraq might break out of UN sanctions and reveal a more substantial capability than now seems likely. Paradoxically, such an Iraqi capability would help to legitimize Iran and Israel's nuclear, biological, and chemical programs and the escalation to the use of such weapons.

Iraq might use such weapons through proxies or in covert attacks with some degree of plausible deniability. Terrorism and unconventional warfare would be far more intimidating if they made use of weapons of mass destruction.

The Problem of Terrorism

The subject of terrorism presents a host of issues. It is often difficult to distinguish terrorism from unconventional or proxy warfare, and one person's terrorist is another person's free - dom fighter. Failed regimes create their own violent opposition through their mistreatment of minorities, repression, and eco- nomic failures. These pressures interact in the Gulf with the economic costs of war and revolution, and with a broad failure to offer Gulf youth the education, job opportunities, and social roles necessary to fully integrate one of the world's youngest and most rapidly growing populations into its society. The rentier, or welfare character, of Southern Gulf regimes and economies is rapidly becoming unaffordable, and Islamic ex - tremism is often a natural refuge.

At one level, this is likely to pose at least a low-level con - tinuing threat to the United States and other Western power projection forces and other foreigners in the Gulf as the natu - ral proxies for the regime. This problem is likely to be com - pounded by the dismal quality of the efforts of Southern Gulf regimes to explain their own security policies to their peoples or the reasons for the United States and Western presence. At another level, those dispossessed and discriminated against are likely to use violence directly against their regimes and become the natural proxies of Iran and Iraq. This is particu - larly true in countries where royal families deny the legitimacy of their grievances, blame the problem on other states, and/or fail to respond to demands for broader political participation.

Generally, these threats will only be serious if Southern Gulf regimes consistently fail their peoples and attempt to live in a world of patriarchal illusions. The bad news is that there will be many bombings and killings in the years to come. The good news is that they should be as containable as those in other parts of the world if regimes transform their good inten - tions regarding economic and social reform into actions, and learn that they must communicate far more effectively with their own people. As bad as future embassy bombings and Al Khobars may be, they will only be fatal to Gulf security if the Gulf's problems are allowed to escalate out of control, some - thing that currently seems improbable.

The key wild card is the possible use of weapons of mass destruction. Iran and Iraq have the option of exploiting a wide range of unconventional delivery methods that are far less expensive, difficult, and detectable than most of the previous delivery systems. In addition, Iraq may be able to use other radical nations or groups that either sympathize with it or would strike against Iraq's enemies for their own reasons.

Once again, there is no way to determine what Iran and Iraq will or will not plan in the future. Their official attitude toward terrorism is the usual one of denial, but this has scarcely proved to be the reality in the past. Further, Iran and Iraq's efforts may well be improvised and reactive, suddenly escalat- ing the scale of its use of unconventional warfare/terrorism in reaction to a given contingency or the failure of its military forces. This makes any effort to characterize their use of such delivery methods purely speculative, whether in terms of warning against such threats or denying their existence.

What is clear is that such attacks are technically feasible and could offer Iran and Iraq significant advantages in a wide range of scenarios. Many of the attacks may seem to borrow plots from bad spy novels and science fiction, but all of the scenarios are at least technically possible. These scenarios also illustrate the fact that Iraq does not need sophisticated military delivery systems or highly lethal weapons of mass destruction, but can use terrorism to pose existential threats, complex mixes of weapons of mass destruction, and mix ter - rorism with elements of covert action and deniability.

The danger of such scenarios is that they tend to overstate Iran and Iraq's willingness turn to extreme forms of terror, the readiness of proxies to risk dying, and Iran and Iraq's ability to undetectably execute complex attacks. At the same time, the scenarios are not difficult to execute, and only a few re - quire large numbers of people and complex technical activity.

The actions of Aum Shinrikyo have already shown that it can be extremely difficult to characterize the level of extrem - ism and capability for sophisticated action by a given group until it has committed at least one act of terror. The cell structure used by the violent elements of most Middle Eastern extremist groups tends to encourage the creation of compart - mented groups with different and unpredictable commitments to violence. At the same time, the loose and informal chain of contacts between extremist movements, known terrorist groups, and radical governments like Iran creates the possibility of random or unpredictable transfers of technology or weapons. There are many possibilities and no clear probabilities.

Chapter 3

Arab Perspectives on Middle Eastern Security

Ibrahim A. Karawan

For a long time, Middle Eastern security was closely tied in the strategic perceptions of that region to the prospects of a peaceful settlement of the conflict between the Arab states and Israel. While most analysts agree there is no military solution to that protracted conflict and, thus, no realistic al - ternative to a negotiated settlement of the Arab-Israeli conflict, few observers are inclined to believe there will be such a set - tlement in the near future. The euphoria about a looming Middle East peace created by the historic handshake between Yassir Arafat and Yitzhak Rabin in front of the White House in September 1993 has disappeared. Policy makers and opinion makers on all sides have referred to the peace process as passing through a critical stage. [1] In March 1998, Ahmed Ab - del Rahman, secretary-general of the cabinet of the Palestin - ian authority, has indeed gone considerably further when he announced the death of the peace process despite the absence of an official burial or a memorial service.[2]

Even if the most appropriate term in describing the current shape of the peace process turns out to be "stalemate," such a state should not be expected to end soon, particularly since the contested issues in the final status talks between the Palestinians and Israel such as the future of Jerusalem, secu - rity, sovereignty, borders, water, and the refugee problems are decidedly the most complicated and the thorniest issues in the Arab-Israeli conflict.[3]

Nothing illustrates the stalemate of the peace process more than the freezing of the normalization of relations between Arab states and Israel. Almost all of the Arab states have put any trade projects or economic cooperation with Israel on an indefinite hold. The public opinion in these countries is widely in favor of such a policy position. Not surprisingly, a confer - ence that met in Doha, Qatar, in November 1997 with the primary intention of promoting Arab-Israeli economic cooperation as the foundation for regional peace has ended in failure despite the persistent efforts by the United States to make that economic conference successful.[4]

While a stalemate is not exactly a new or unheard of phe - nomenon on the Middle Eastern regional level, the dramatic weakening of all the earlier hopes and expectations of peace has created a setting in which most observers are no longer talking about visions of Middle Eastern economic integration and normalization. Instead, pessimistic scenarios of low intensity conflict, acts of terrorism, possible military confrontations over Lebanon and between Syria and Israel, and attempts at the proliferation of weapons of mass destruction (WMD) have been gaining greater attention. While a general regional war remains unlikely, the continuation of the state of no war and no peace in the region could trigger new and dangerous clashes and rounds of violence. The political discourse in Arab countries during the last few years, and particularly since the mid-1990s, reflects an emphasis on these specific strategic challenges. It is the objective of this author to examine such a mind-set, assess the major security challenges facing the Arab world, and the best options for dealing with them as seen by Arab policy makers and policy analysts.

The Strategic Environment

Before going any further, it may be useful to make three important points about the Arab strategic environment. First, analysis of the strategic perceptions in the Arab world reveals that the option of a general war against Israel is not seen as feasible. Egypt and Jordan's disengagement from the conflict with Israel or defection from the war equation with the Jewish state is a strategic development that is not considered as a transient or short-term reality. Rather, these two crucial fronts are widely seen as frozen for many years to come.

Military institutions in what used to be called "Arab con - frontation states" are among the strongest forces calling for the avoidance of pursuing the military option against Israel as much as possible. These institutions developed a healthy ap - preciation of Israel's military might and capabilities; and, hence, they are not ready for pursuing adventuristic or reck -

less security policies vis-à-vis the Jewish state. In fact, both the 1967 and 1973 wars demonstrated not only the utility but also the limits of any massive resort to the military options. While Israel achieved a major military victory over its Arab adversaries in 1967, it was not able to secure peace with them. On the contrary, the Arab's defeat made them more determined to strike back. Although Egypt and Syria per - formed much better in the 1973 war than in the 1967 war and managed to surprise Israeli forces at first, the end of the war witnessed very serious Israeli pressures against Egyptian and Syrian forces despite the allocation of huge resources for the war effort and intensive training of their military over the previous six years.

Moreover, Arab economic elites see any large-scale regional clashes as not conducive to economic development or for ex - pecting a significant inflow of foreign capital and investment into Arab countries. Even for countries like Syria that did not achieve much progress in economic liberalization, particularly after the demise of its Soviet ally, a large-scale military con - frontation by itself with Israel, in a de facto alliance with Turkey, would be seen as an invitation for a disaster that the Syrian political leadership must avoid at all costs. [5] Another massive Syrian defeat would result in a decline of Syria's relative power vis-à-vis other actors in the region and would also undermine the Syrian regime's political legitimacy in the eyes of its own society.[6]

Second, Arab countries are not equally worried about their own strategic interactions with Israel. Syria has sharper pre - occupation with the conflict with Israel than, for instance, Kuwait, which is concerned with threats against its territory and interests. Saudi Arabia keeps watchful eyes on Iraq and Iran at the same time. Similarly, the Israeli problem has been secondary for the United Arab Emirates has been preoccupied in a territorial conflict with Iran. The same is true for Morocco which worries about the Western Sahara problem and the territorial tensions along its borders with Algeria.[7]

In other words, in the contemporary Arab world, the logic of the territorial state has been gaining more influence and ad - herents at the expense of transnational doctrines, whether the Arab nationalist doctrine or pan-Islamist causes. [8] Even with regard to the Turkish-Israeli military cooperation that worried Syria and made her try to mobilize Arab support, the positions of Arab states varied significantly.[9] According to Ali Dessouki, a prominent Egyptian political scientist, "Arab reactions [have] varied from tacit approval, to downright silence, to expression of reservation, and to seeing it as a threat."[10] This development came against the backdrop of the earlier predictions of the withering away of the Arab states as artificial entities created by colonial powers. However, the Arab multistate system has proven to be more resilient than was anticipated.[11]

The record of failures and defeats of those political regimes who have proclaimed themselves as pan-Arabists and who have striven to transform the Arab world in their image have been depressingly vast. No matter what their leaders say in paying homage to their doctrines, it is the pursuit of state interests and, more importantly, the regime interests that guides their behavior. One manifestation of that trend has been the outbreak of Arab-Arab conflicts that reached the point of military clashes.[12]

Third, not all the security threats to Arab states are external. For sometime, analysts have tended to perceive national security in light of the military threats originating from sources beyond state boundaries. According to such a neorealist outlook, "threats arising from outside a state are some - what more dangerous to its security than threats that arise within it."[13] In many Arab countries plagued with ethnic ten - sions, economic hardships, violent opposition to regime exist - ence, and threats to the life and wealth of its rulers, domestic threats to regime security loom large and are linked often to outside powers.

Under such conditions, national security tends to be equated with regime security. [14] One strategy of dealing with severe domestic threats is to make major shifts of external behavior or security and foreign policies to ameliorate these threats. The Egyptian and the Palestinian restructuring their policies towards Israel provides examples of such preservative linkage between acute domestic tensions and an accommodationist international behavior, or the appeasement of an external threat to contain more pressing internal threats to state core interests or regime security.[15]

During the 1980s and the 1990s, Arab states such as Egypt, Algeria, Saudi Arabia, and Yemen suffered from terrorism that adversely affected their economies and their internal stability. Putting an end to terrorism became a major policy objective of these states. The reasons are not difficult to identify. After all, terrorists often target the leaders of these regimes whom they perceive as agents of imperialism and Zionism.[16] They also strive to undermine what they consider to be the fundamental foundation of state order which is the sense of awe towards it and to disrupt revenue-generating institutions. In doing that, some terrorists like those trained in the Afghan war, have been able to launch destructive and sophisticated operations that require an extensive infrastructure, logistical support, and elaborate planning.[17]

Much has been said lately about the declining number of members of terrorist organizations . But even if this assessment turns out to be factually true, perceptions of the dangers posed by terrorist groups will persist. Terrorism in the Middle East has not been based on the logic of strength in numbers. A few cadres from Hamas and the Islamic Jihad managed to create a climate of fear and greater worry about security in Israel during the few first months of 1996, a climate that enhanced the electoral chances of Benyamin Netanyahu in Israel. Six militant Islamists managed by attacking and killing tens of tourists in Luxor to seriously undermine the revenues from tourism in Egypt for about a year.

For a long time, many perceived the Middle East as an area that is important both geostrategically and geoeconomically but as unchanging along political and cultural lines, and, thus, insulated against significant transformations. The start of the Arab-Israeli peace and rise of considerable threats against regimes, supposed for long to be stable, had challenged this outlook. Soon after the onset of the Arab-Israeli peace process, some analysts had anticipated a decisive rupture with the past through a new Middle East marked by war termination, regional peace, and economic interdependence. The difficulties of translating this vision into tangible realities are unmistakable.

The Nuclear Dimension

The fact the Middle East has not been among the success stories in curbing the spread of nuclear weapons is not surprising. A number of its regional powers aspired to possess nuclear weapons, and Israel is one of a few undeclared nu - clear powers in the world.[18] The complexity of the Arab-Israeli conflict, its protracted nature, multidimensional levels, and the bitter legacies it has created could help us understand why. The obstacles facing the regional actors in reaching a consensus regarding the nuclear issue are numerous, and the minimum level of confidence between these actors to overcome such obstacles is just simply not there.[19]

There are additional conflicts in the Middle East that fur - ther complicate reaching a consensus on the nuclear issue. The conflict in the Persian Gulf is one important example of these conflicts that influence perceptions and interactions, not only in that subregion but also beyond the boundaries of the Gulf itself. The challenges facing a viable settlement of nuclear issues are daunting. Establishing a nuclear-weapons-free zone (NWFZ) in the Middle East similar to other regions, as advocated by many Arab states, involves two difficult and in - terrelated tasks, namely rolling back the Israeli nuclear weapons program and freezing the nonnuclear status of the other regional actors.[20]

Most Middle East observers agree the region has one sole nuclear power, Israel. Many use such terms as *protonuclear, opacity*, the *bomb in the basement*, and the *policy of opaqueness*.[21] There is little doubt about Israel's possession of a nu - clear arsenal and the means of delivering nuclear devices to their targets. Regardless of Israel's refusal to acknowledge its nuclear capability, such a capability has become widely recognized, particularly after the information provided by the Israeli technician Mordecai Vannunu in 1986. Policy makers in the surrounding countries and their societies cannot afford to ig - nore this consideration.

For obvious reasons, most of the discussions about the nu - clear factor in the Middle East tend to be contentious and polemical in content and style. From the start, I would like to make two precautionary points. [22] First, this writer does not argue that the Israeli decision to acquire a nuclear capability was at that time an imprudent step. The features of the re - gional setting in the late 1950s and early 1960s as perceived by Israel's core elite underlined the importance of acquiring a nonconventional deterrence. Both Israel's demonstration of preponderance of conventional power and perceptions of Arab leaders that it had nuclear capability put significant con - straints on those leaders' conduct vis-à-vis the Jewish state.

However, one should not minimize the significance of trans - formations on the regional level—changes that could make the so-called two hundred bombs in the basement approach go beyond the outer limits of its strategic utility. What might have been useful three or four decades ago is not necessarily useful today, and may not be useful in the future. Rather, it might accelerate the proliferation of nuclear weapons because some Arab states in addition to the Islamic Republic of Iran are likely to perceive the Israeli nuclear monopoly as threatening enough actually to warrant developing their own weapons of mass destruction and missile programs. [23] In the case of Iran, for instance, the launching of Shehab 3 missile on 28 July 1998 and the possible launching of the Shehab 4 me - dium-range missile that can each bring all of Israel within Tehran's striking distance illustrates the type of regional reactions, serious tensions, and arms races that could result.[24]

Second, the time frame of any policy restructuring on Is - rael's part is one of the most important variables to be taken into consideration. Obviously, a dramatic change in Israel's position regarding the Nonproliferation Treaty (NPT) and mak - ing the Middle East a NWFZ cannot happen overnight. As the decision to go nuclear was influenced by the protracted state of the war in the region, any decision to move in the opposite direction, namely denuclearization, has to be tied to a Middle East peace and its consolidation. Nonetheless, such a move should not be made conditional on having all Arab and Is - lamic countries sign peace treaties and maintain normal rela - tions with Israel for some years before Israel agrees to move on the nuclear issue.

For example, the Israeli position stipulating that all Middle Eastern countries, including the Islamic Republic of Iran, must sign peace treaties and also maintain normal relations with Israel for at least two years before negotiating a change in Israel's current policy on the nuclear issue is viewed in the Arab world as an example of an Israeli determination to enjoy nuclear monopoly in the region for a very long time. One does not necessarily have to be an Arab radical to reach such conclusions. Even those analysts in the Arab world who accepted ending the Arab conflict with Israel, such as Mohamed Sid-Ahmed, Abdel Moneim Said and Saad Eddin Ibrahim, wonder if this is not an impossible condition. Would Pakistan with its so-called Islamic bomb be considered as a real or potential source of threat to Israel? If Pakistan has pursued the nuclear option against the backdrop of its conflict with India who, in turn, has been worried about China and Pakistan, then would a solution to the conflict in South Asia be a prerequisite for a significant modification of Israel's position with regard to nu - clear weapons?

The Israeli position about not being the first country to introduce nuclear weapons in the Middle East is unconvinc ing. Why? Because the logic of the so-called "constructive ambiguity" has ended its usefulness. Other states in the region look at Israel's nuclear capability as a strategic fact and not as an analytic proposition. Thus, the current Israeli position is nei - ther constructive nor ambiguous. Instead of achieving desired stabilization, the current Israeli stand and the interactions resulting from it are likely to lead to more destabilization and to a determined drive by other regional actors to acquire a nuclear capability in addition to more chemical and biological weapons. There is the need for dialogue about the dangers of nuclearization in the Middle East in a manner that requires all parties, including Israel, to reassess their long held positions.

What should guide such a reassessment? First is the con - cept of nondiscrimination among states and establishing one standard of state behavior and verification requirements. While regions have their own specificity, there should not be two sets of standards of what is permissible and what is not permissible: one standard for democracies and another for nondemocratic states. After all, the only country in history that used nuclear weapons against their adversary's cities and civilians is a democratic country, strongly associated with notions of Lockean liberalism.

When it comes to the Middle East, arguments about the virtues and necessity of discrimination are used to make the case for Israel exceptionalism. Some argue that the Middle East is an exceptional case due to structural security dilem - mas that involve the Arab-Muslim coalition against Israel. Those who believe so also tell us that Israel is an exceptional case not only because of its identity, but also due to its politi - cal system, which is characterized by democracy and account - ability. This argument, dubbed as *dual exceptionalism*, means that Israel has to continue to be the exception in the region in terms of possessing nuclear capability. In short, the Middle East has to become a NWFZ with one exception, which is happening now.

Second is the issue of sequencing and priorities, which poses the question of causes and effects. Does the estab - lishment of a NWFZ build regional confidence and security, or does this result from peace, confidence, and a sense of secu - rity? In the Middle East, this is not a theoretical issue. While Egypt argues that clear progress regarding the nuclear issue must precede or be parallel to progress in a political settle - ment, Israel argues that security and successful confidence-building measures must come first. This poses a dilemma, particularly when we consider that the leaders on both sides have to convince their publics about a change in the inten - tions and policies of the other side before being able to move towards a compromise.

Third, what is the best approach to bring about the estab - lishment of a NWFZ in the Middle East? How can a NWFZ be created given the characteristics of the regional situation? What lessons can be learned from successful cases in other regions? How can we assess the merits and demerits of the regional versus global approaches? Can a NWFZ best be insti-tuted via policy pressure or political persuasion? These are controversial issues, though it seems that arm-twisting meth - ods when it comes to denuclearization are not likely to pro - duce the most positive results. The record of such tactics in dealing with actors aspiring to join "the nuclear club" is am - biguous. Regional approaches may have promise because they avoid the accusation of international imposition. However, for the regional approaches to be effective and legitimate, they should not endorse and perpetuate a privileged position for one regional actor, particularly if that actor has an acknow - ledged preponderance of conventional military power and, so far, a monopoly of nuclear power.

Changes in the Regional Setting

Israel prefers to focus on the regional approaches and tends to be concerned about international channels or organizations influenced by a pro-Arab "numerical majority." Israel also ar - gues it cannot rely on the Nonproliferation Treaty, which was extended indefinitely in May 1995. Moreover, it stresses that the verification mechanisms of the International Atomic En - ergy Agency are dangerously inadequate as shown by recent cases in Iraq and North Korea, and accordingly, regional ap - proaches and solutions must be given priority.

But an approach that merits the word "regional" must not ignore important regional transformations. Thus, we should have a regional outlook that captures the changes in the re - gional setting. For most Arab actors, the conflict with Israel is no longer about its *wujud* or "existence" but about its *hudud* or "borders." This policy shift did not obviously result from an abrupt normative change of attitudes unconnected to political realities. It has stemmed from experience, the essence of which is that Israel is in the Middle East to stay, and that there is no viable military solution to the Arab-Israeli conflict.

Hafiz al-Assad; Yassir Arafat; King Abdullah II; King Fahd; President Hosni Mubarak; leaders of Tunisia, Morocco, and Algeria; and the Gulf Cooperation Council (GCC) countries differ in their own political readings of regional and international settings. However, they all have realized the futility of any strategy that relies on military power against Israel. Needless to say, if one compares such a position with the famous three Arab "noes" (no peace, no recognition, and no negotiations with Israel) adopted by the Arab summit in Khartoum in 1967, the significance of that alteration of policy should be easy to appreciate. It belongs to the category of what international relations scholars call foreign policy restructuring. The peace process is far from success and serious difficulties remain, but it would be a mistake to conclude that nothing of significance has happened in the Middle East.

The threats associated with terrorism are not ones that nu - clear weapons are useful to deal with. Hizbollah, Hamas, and Islamic Jihad leaders did not have doubts about Israeli nu - clear capability. But this did not prevent or deter them from launching attacks against Israeli targets, knowing full well that Israel could not have used its nuclear weapons against them near its own northern borders. Links with countries like Syria and Iran are well established. However, Israel could not use the threat of nuclear weapons to compel these two states to stop backing such attacks. Thus, the *bomb in the basement* is not useful against the most frequent kind of threat or vis-à-vis nearby states which give the terrorist groups backing, funding, or shelter.

It has been argued that the case of Iraq's behavior in Janu- ary and February 1991 demonstrated the utility of having an Israeli nuclear option in forcing Iraq not to use its chemical weapons against Israel. Digging into Saddam Hussein's inten - tions is a hazardous exercise in crystal-ball gazing, to say the least. What remains obvious is that Saddam warned ahead of time that if Iraq was attacked, he would launch Scud missiles against Israel and did so despite knowing about Israel's con - siderable nuclear arsenal. In other words, Saddam was not deterred. When Israel was reportedly on the verge of a re - sponse (search and destroy air missions), it considered con - ventional weapons. It is likely that America's threat to use unconventional weapons if Iraq used chemical weapons had reinforced the Iraqi inclination not to use such weapons un - less attacked with weapons of mass destruction.

Iran's intentions have been suspect when it comes to the nuclear issue. Estimates vary regarding the time it would need and the specific conditions necessary for Iran to develop its own nuclear capability. Many are inclined to see another ex - perience similar to that of Iraq and to conclude that Iran may display verbal moderation on nuclear issues in front of inter - national organizations while being intent on developing its own nuclear weapons program. However, if reports about an active nuclear program by Iran were true, it would be fair to assume that the Iranians want to succeed. In that regard, their model would be Israel which succeeded, not Iraq which failed, and had as a result of its defeat an intrusive inspection regime over its military sites and bases.

What Is To Be Done?

Most Arab states favor making the Middle East a NWFZ and consider this option superior to other available courses of action. One can identify two alternatives. One favors the status quo, and according to it Israel must remain the only regional nuclear power for the foreseeable future. Advocates of this view argue that it is good not only for Israel but also for the region. Here we have a regional version of the theory of hegemonic stability. Some argue this would be welcome by the Arab countries in the Gulf region who are worried about Iraq or Iran. Israel's nuclear umbrella can provide unlimited secu - rity for them, and regional stability in the entire Middle East would be enhanced as a result.

This argument has many weaknesses. It ignores the impact of domestic politics in Arab countries. Even authoritarian re - gimes in the Arab world have certain domestic politics. There are strident discussions in Arab political life about Israel's assured monopoly of nuclear weapons and the strategic risks involved in allowing such a monopoly to continue. In fact, retired generals who belong to or sympathize with opposition forces provide the general membership and opposition news - papers with alarming accounts of the expansion of Israel's nuclear arsenal. They argue Israel behaves on the assumption that its conflict with the Arabs is going to continue, while Arab regimes act as if that conflict has become a thing of the past. This can be clearly seen in Egypt and Jordan and other Arab countries where the mass media, whether official or not, de - nounce US insistence on denying Arab states any nuclear option while de facto sanctioning or endorsing Israel's posses - sion of a large nuclear arsenal.

The more political liberalization takes hold in the Arab world, the greater the likelihood that more or wider segments of Arab public opinion will reject Israel's nuclear monopoly. Accord - ingly, many Arab regimes will be pressured to take a stronger stand against the Israeli nuclear monopoly, to refrain from signing treaties banning chemical weapons, or to pursue nuclear options. Advocacy of such actions may not come only from the ranks of the opposition but also from within the institutional structure of some Arab states. When it comes to dealing with Israeli "nuclear file," the Foreign Ministry and Defence Ministry in Egypt are examples. While they accept that Israel has a democratic system, they argue democratic elections can bring extremists to power and they see Likud and Netanyahu in Israeli politics as a confirmation of that outlook.

Pro-Western Arab regimes will not venture to rely on an Israeli nuclear umbrella while they can be protected by the United States when faced with extreme danger. If that happens, they will try to make sure, as they did during the war to liberate Kuwait, that Israel does not intervene militarily and, thus greatly complicate matters for them politically on the domestic and regional levels.

The other alternative is based on the Waltzian notion of the stabilizing effects of nuclear weapons or "the more the better" for regional order and stable deterrence. [25] To put it rather crudely, from such a perspective, it is better to have a Middle East with nuclear weapons on all or most sides of its conflicts, than to have an area ridden with recurrent costly wars but with no nuclear weapons. There are many weaknesses in this argument. Examples are the inapplicability of the Soviet-American model to the Middle East, the serious risks involved in nuclear proliferation, and the fact that the chances of a general war in the Middle East have been reduced after Egypt opted out of the war equation in the late 1970s.

For years, Egypt has been advocating the establishment of a NWFZ. As Egypt embarked on a settlement with Israel in 1974, it raised this issue before the General Assembly of the United Nations. President Hosni Mubarak suggested in 1990 establishing a zone free of weapons of mass destruction in the Middle East.[26] Egypt accepted the notion that this process would require several years for confidence-building as well as institution-building purposes and a verification regime that would go beyond procedures described in the Nonproliferation Treaty to ensure strict compliance by the member states which should have equal rights and responsibilities.[27]

To conclude, the threat of nuclear proliferation remains real in the Middle East. But it is not likely to be the type of proliferation that can lead to greater regional stability. On the other hand, nonproliferation of WMD can generate more fears and insecurity in the region, possibly with some disastrous consequences. Even the countries that have made peace with Israel, as shown in the case of Egypt and Jordan, do not want to be reduced to mere helpless entities under the Israeli nu - clear dominance. Even if their leaders were ready to accept that many in state institutions, particularly in the military, will continue to see their relations with Israel in competitive terms. Their societies and their elites will find Israel's nuclear capability threatening and will continue to pressure for con - fronting Israeli nuclear monopoly. While abolishing nuclear weapons immediately in the Middle East with no exceptions whatsoever is unrealistic, moving seriously in the direction of eliminating nuclear threats is necessary for security and sta - bility in that strategic region. There is no better alternative.

Notes

1. See the Washington Institute for Near East Policy, 1998 Soref Symposium, "The Oslo Impasse: Where Do We Go From Here?" 6-7 May 1998.

2. International Institute for Strategic Studies, *Strategic Survey, 1997–1998* (Oxford: Oxford University Press, 1998), 144.

3. Shibley Telhami and Lawrence Velte, *The Arab-Israeli Peace Process: Assessing the Cost of Failure* (Strategic Studies Institute, US Army War College, June 1997).

4. Joel Beinin, "The Demise of the Oslo Process," MERIP Report, March 1999.

5. Scott Peterson, "Wild Card in Middle East Peace: Syria," *Christian Science Monitor,* 24 September 1997.

6. Ibrahim A. Karawan, "Arab Dilemmas in the 1990s: Breaking Taboos and Searching for Signposts," *Middle East Journal* 48, no. 3 (May 1994): 433–54.

7. Saleh al-Mani, "Of Security and Threat: Saudi Arabia's Perceptions," *Journal of South Asian and Middle Eastern Studies* 20, no. 1 (Fall 1996); and Hassan al-Alkim, "The Islands' Question: UAE Perspective," paper presented at the Gulf 2000 Project Conference, Columbia University, Castelgandolfo, Italy, 26–30 July 1998; and Sean Foley, "UAE: Political Issues and Security Dilemmas," *Middle East Review of International Affairs* 3, no. 1 (March 1998).

8. Abdel Monem Said Aly, "The Shattered Consensus: Arab Perceptions of Security," *International Spectator* 31, no. 4 (October–December 1996): 23–52.

9. Dov Waxman, "Turkey and Israel: A New Balance in the Middle East," *Washington Quarterly* 22, no. 1 (Winter 1999): 25–32. See articles in the pro *Syrian al-Safir* (Beirut), 10 October 1998 and in *al-Itihad* (United Arab Emirates), 14 October 1998.

10. As quoted by CAN, Nicosia, 30 March 1999. See Mahmoud 'Awad, "Syria and Turkey: Deficient Answers," *al-Hayat*, 30 October 1998, 15.

11. See Keith Krause, "Insecurity and State Formation in the Global Military Order: The Middle Eastern Case," *European Journal of International Relations* 2, no. 3 (1996): 319–54; and Karawan, "The Withering Away of the Arab State: Reflections on A Premature Memorial Service," paper presented to the international conference marking the 350th anniversary of the peace of Westphalia, Enschede, the Netherlands, 16–19 July 1998.

12. Mohamed Abdel-Salam, *Intra-Arab Conflicts,* Center for Political and Strategic Studies al-Ahram Foundation, Cairo, no. 23, 1995.

13. Richard Ullman, "Redefining Security," *International Security* 8, no. 1 (Summer 1983): 19.

14. Bahgat Korany, Paul Noble, Rex Brynen, eds., *The Many Faces of National Security in the Arab World* (New York: St. Martin's Press, 1993); and with specific reference to Syria see Muhammad Muslih, "Asad's Foreign Policy Strategy," *Critique* (Spring 1998): 66–68.

15. See Steven David, *Choosing Sides: Alignment and Realignment in the Third World* (Baltimore: Johns Hopkins University Press, 1991); Michael Barnett and Jack Levy, "The Domestic Sources of Alliances and Alignment," *International Organization* 45, no. 3 (Summer 1991): 369–95.

16. See an interview with the Islamic group leader, Rifa'I Taha in *al-Quds al-'Arabi* (London), 15 August 1998, 3; and Amira Hass, "What the PA Fears: Terrorism," *Ha'aretz,* 13 April 1998.

17. Radwan al-Sayyed, "The Arab Afghans Again," *al-Safir,* 6 August 1998; and *al-Safir,* 12 August 1998.

18. For a comprehensive review see Anthony Cordesman, *Military Balance in the Middle East: Weapons of Mass Destruction,* Center for Strategic and International Studies, March 1999.

19. See William Dowdy, "Nuclear Proliferation Issues and Prospects in the Middle East," in *Pulling Back from the Nuclear Brink: Reducing and Countering Nuclear Threats,* ed. Barry Schneider and William Dowdy (London: Frank Cass, 1998), 136–47; Shai Feldman, *Nuclear Weapons and Arms Control in the Middle East* (Cambridge: MIT Press, 1998); and for a different perspective see Hans-Heinrich Wrede, "Applicability of the CSCE Experience to the Middle Eastern Conflict Area," *Jerusalem Journal of International Relations* 14, no. 2 (1992): 114–22.

20. John Brook Wolfsthal, "Nuclear-Weapon-Free Zones: Coming of Age," *Arms Control Today,* March 1993, 7.

21. See Shai Feldman, *Israeli Nuclear Deterrence* (New York: Columbia University Press, 1982); Benjamin Frankel, *Opaque Nuclear Proliferation* (London: Frank Cass, 1991); Shlomo Aronson with Oded Brosh, *The Politics and Strategy of Nuclear Weapons in the Middle East: Opacity, Theory, and Reality, 1960–1991* (Albany: State University of New York Press, 1992); and Etel Solingen, "The Domestic Sources of Regional Regimes: The Evolution of Nuclear Ambiguity in the Middle East," *International Studies Quarterly,* June 1994, 305–37.

22. The ideas of this part overlap with parts of Karawan, "The Case for a Nuclear Weapon Free Zone in the Middle East," in Ramesh Thakur, *Nuclear Weapons-Free Zones* (London: Macmillan Press, 1998), particularly 186–91. For counter arguments see Gerald Steinberg, "The Obstacles to a Middle East Nuclear-Weapon-Free Zone," in Ramesh Thakur, *Nuclear Weapons-Free Zones* (London: Macmillan Press, 1998), 194–209.

23. For a good discussion of Iran's threat perceptions see Eric Arnett, "Reassurance versus Deterrence: Expanding Iranian Participation in Confidence-Building Measures," *Security Dialogue* 29, no. 4 (1998): 435–47.

24. Farhat Taj, "Iranian Test-Firing of Shihab-III Missile," *The Frontier Post,* 7 August 1998.

25. See a study influenced by that perspective, Shai Feldman, "Middle East Nuclear Stability," *Journal of International Affairs* 49, no. 1 (Summer 1995): 205–30.

26. On Egypt's position see Mahmoud Karem, *A Nuclear-Weapons-Free Zone in the Middle East: Problems and Prospects* (New York: Greenwood Press, 1988); and Mohamed Shaker, *Prospects for Establishing a Zone Free of Weapons of Mass Destruction in the Middle East* (Lawrence Livermore National Laboratory, October 1994).

27. See Efraim Karsh and Yezid Sayigh, "A Cooperative Approach to Arab-Israeli Security," *Survival* 36, no. 1 (Spring 1994): 121–25.

Chapter 4

Regional Security and Arms Control in the Middle East
The Nuclear Dimension

Avner Cohen

After decades of bloody conflict between Arabs and Jews in the Middle East, the trend of history may have reversed itself. Since the mid- to late 1970s, following the war that brought Arabs and Israelis nearest to the nuclear brink in 1973, the region has seemed to favor reconciliation over the continu - ation of the conflict, negotiation over hostilities, and peace over war. Notwithstanding present setbacks, one can still no - tice a long-term trend in the Arab world to accept Israel as a neighbor that must be reckoned with. In parallel, Israelis have subscribed to the idea and reality of trading land for peace, in one form or another.

Resolving a century-old conflict, however, has proved to be immensely difficult, slow, and painful. Almost every step for - ward has been met with setbacks and frustration. The ever-present conflict has shaped the mind-set and identity of both Arabs and Israelis. This mind-set is deeply rooted in images and perceptions of threat and enmity—"us" versus "them"—compounded by historical memories of trauma and catastrophe. One cannot underestimate the lasting power of these mind-sets; they shape the political reality of the region.

The assassination of the prime minister who boldly started the Oslo process, the wave of terrorist acts aimed to sabotage it, and, subsequently, the election of a new prime minister Netauyahu wholeheartedly opposed to the philosophy behind that process, demonstrates the lasting power of conflict in the Middle East. Old habits die hard.

On the Israeli side, the conflict has cultivated a siege men - tality. Israel became a "garrison state" as a result of belliger - ent Arab rhetoric concerning the "liberation of Palestine" and "throwing the Jews into the sea," compounded by the trauma and lessons of the holocaust. In response to a perceived exis -

tential threat, a philosophy of self-reliance has emerged. On the Arab side, Zionism has been perceived as aggressive, ex - pansive, and brutal, as evidenced by the catastrophe of 1948. Seeing themselves as victims of Zionist aggression, Arab states have refused to recognize Israel, keeping alive the hope that one day this historical injustice will be corrected. Over - arching this symbolic and psycho-cultural reality is the fact that permanent geopolitical asymmetries exist between the parties of the Arab-Israeli conflict.

Weapons of mass destruction (WMD), of which nuclear weapons are the ultimate manifestation, have played pro - found, but often tacit, roles (symbolic and actual) in both heightening and mediating the dynamics of the Arab-Israeli conflict. The apocalyptic shadow of the bomb has hovered over the Arab-Israeli conflict for almost two generations. Out of its existential anxiety about its security and its "self-reliant" phi- losophy, Israel was the first to rush to "get" the bomb. Israel did not seek its nuclear capability for the sake of hegemonic aspirations or national prestige. Instead, David Ben Gurion's interest in these weapons, highlighted by his decision in the mid-to-late 1950s to develop an independent nuclear deter - rent, was seen as addressing the sacred matter of national survival, the ultimate way to balance the fundamental geopo - litical asymmetries in Arab-Israeli conventional military power.[1] The bomb was to be Israel's ultimate insurance policy, enabling Israel to inflict a holocaust on its enemies to prevent another holocaust on Israel. Fearing both regional and global repercussions, Israel at first kept its quest secret. Although it acquired a nuclear option sometime in the late 1960s, Israel has not declared, tested, or made any other visible use of this option, resulting in an "opaque" nuclear policy.[2]

The nuclear age opened in the Middle East with a whimper. While Israel maintained its secrecy, the Arab states, including Egypt, did not place Israel's secret nuclear project high on their international agenda. [3] Nobody knew that, during the 1967 crisis, Israel had slapped together the ultimate weapon.[4] By 1970 the basic facts became known: The Israelis had the bomb; the Arabs did not. This did not deter the Arabs from waging another bloody war in 1973, a war designed to change the status quo. A decade later, with the advent of Iraq's re -

gional aspirations, the nuclear issue became more prominent on the Arab-Israeli agenda.

Since the mid to late 1970s, Iraq, under Saddam Hussein , has vigorously pursued WMD programs. To prevent this, in 1981, Israel bombed and destroyed the Iraqi Osiraq reactor. [5] The attack on Osiraq was the first time that nuclear programs triggered an escalation of the Arab-Israel conflict. [6] Although Iraq, occupied at the time with its war with Iran, did not retaliate against Israel, it also did not give up its WMD program. By the late 1980s, Iraq had resumed its vigorous pursuit of un - conventional weaponry. For Saddam, nuclear weapons are the ultimate symbol of defiance, prestige, technological achievement, and power projection. His pursuit, however, ended with a bang. The Persian Gulf War was, to a degree, about denying Iraq access to the destructive capabilities of WMD (nuclear weapons in particular) as the terms for the Gulf War cease-fire indicated.

It was primarily the experience with Iraq, and the end of the cold war, that shifted the discourse from nuclear weapons to the broader category of WMD . Iraq had used chemical weap - ons against Iranian troops during the 1980–88 Iran-Iraq war and against its own Kurdish civilian population in 1988. Iraq had also threatened to use chemical weapons against Israel ("burning half [of] Israel"), if Israel launched a preemptive strike against "strategic sites" in Iraq. [7] Against this back - ground of Iraqi threats and Israeli counterthreats, Egyptian President Hosni Mubarak developed an "initiative" to broaden Egypt's position on the establishment of a nuclear-weapon-free-zone (NWFZ) in the Middle East to cover weapons of mass destruction.[8] The mandate of UN Security Council Resolution 687, which defined the terms of the cease-fire after the Gulf War, called for the dismantlement of Iraq's WMD, so as to "render harmless" Iraq's capabilities to produce them, and to monitor Iraq's compliance. Subsequent resolutions, notably 707 and 715, explicated further the terms of this mandate.[9]

Still, it was the "what-if" specter of a nuclear-armed Iraq that provided the strongest impetus both for the establishment of UNSCOM and for increasing international interest in establishing a full array of nonproliferation tools and modalities, including a mechanism to address issues of regional security and arms control. The reality of a nuclear-armed Israel also deepened the ominous shadows of crisis and war in the Per - sian Gulf in 1990–91. Some believe that if Iraq had not in - vaded Kuwait, a later Iraqi-Israeli confrontation would have been unavoidable.[10] UN Resolution 687 vaguely linked the two: UNSCOM's explicit mandate to eliminate Iraq's nuclear weapons capabilities was loosely based on the longer-term objective to establish a nuclear-weapon-free-zone, indeed a weapons of mass destruction free zone (WMDFZ), in the Mid - dle East. The denuclearization of Iraq was presented as a necessary first step to facilitate regional discussions on ban - ning all WMD in the region.

The period immediately following the American-led defeat of Iraq marked a heady time of regional coordination on regional security and arms control (including the nuclear issue) in the Middle East. The shift in American foreign policy to support regional mechanisms encompassed themes related to both the end of the cold war and the Gulf War: (1) UNSCOM's early revelations on how close Iraq was to developing the bomb; (2) concerns about the transfer of nuclear weapons materials, technology, and expertise from the former Soviet Union; and (3) suspicions about nuclear activities in specific "rogue" countries, especially Iran and North Korea. There was both a growing concern over the nature of the proliferation threat and a realization of the importance of agreements between regional actors as complements to global nonproliferation tools. Fur - thermore, the perception of the United States as the winner of the cold war and the fall of the Soviet Union as the super - power patron of the Arab "rejectionist camp," advanced the notion that the time was ripe for an American-led search for regional arms control. On 29 May 1991, the Bush administra- tion presented its own Middle East Arms Control initiative, which placed special emphasis on regional means to curb the spread of weapons of mass destruction and advanced missiles in the Middle East.[11]

In the region itself, both Israelis and the anti-Saddam Arab coalition seemed to share a common concern about nuclear proliferation and the need to address it on a regional basis. It was understood that a nuclearized conflict between Iraq and Israel had the extremely dangerous potential of engulfing the entire Middle East into an apocalyptic catastrophe. These concerns, often veiled and tacit, contributed significantly to changes in both sides' perceptions of the other.

On the one hand, these concerns have helped to reinforce and advance recognition by the Arab states that, in the nu - clear age, the Arab-Israeli conflict can no longer be resolved through military means. The conflict is too dangerous to per - petuate; therefore, the time has come for the Arabs to "cut a deal" with Israel. The perception of Israel as a superior tech - nological power, as an ineradicable and permanent neighbor in the Middle East that must be dealt with at the negotiation table rather than on the battlefield, gained credence among Arab elites.[12] This did not mean that Arabs were ready to accept the legitimacy of Israel's nuclear program. On the contrary, while many Arabs were concerned about Iraq's nuclear program and ready to see it dismantled, they also insisted that Israel's nuclear program be placed under check. At the outset, a prime motivation for the Arab states to discuss regional security and arms control with Israel was to create a regional forum that would allow them to pressure Israel on the nuclear issue.

On the other hand, the nuclear issue has also played a tacit but important role in moderating fundamental Israeli percep - tions. The recognition that its nuclear monopoly may be vul - nerable, and that it is only a matter of time until a hostile country (Iran, for example) might acquire the bomb, has played an important role in the evolution of Israeli strategic thinking. The lessons of Iraq—particularly the realization that if only Iraq had played its cards right, it could have had the bomb in the early 1990s, without the outside world detecting it—are a gloomy reminder to Israel's leaders that the Israeli nuclear monopoly might not hold indefinitely. In the wake of the Iraqi experience, Israel now has less confidence in its ability to detect and deny unilaterally a nascent hostile nu - clear threat, in Iran or elsewhere, as it did in 1981 in Iraq.[13] Israeli leaders know too well that an Arab-Israeli conflict, in which both sides have access to nuclear weapons, would have catastrophic implications for Israel more than any other country. Indeed, the combination of an arrogant and miscal - culating Arab leader, such as Hussein, and an anxiety-driven Israel with its own ever-present fears of another holocaust, is a recipe for an apocalyptic disaster![14]

Concerns about the introduction of WMD, especially about nuclear weapons, were central to the geopolitical thinking of Israel's late prime minister, Yitzhak Rabin. Rabin saw an in - verse relationship between peace and regional nuclearization, and believed that Iraq's defeat provided a unique "window of opportunity," of perhaps five to 10 years to minimize the threat of hostile nuclearization. During this period, Rabin be - lieved, Israel should contribute to a vigorous nuclear denial strategy via enhanced political and intelligence coordination with friendly states. More fundamentally, Israel should seek peace agreements with all of its immediate neighbors to re - duce support for nuclearization in the Arab world, especially by Iran.[15] Rabin believed that the only way to deny emerging nuclear and other weapons of mass destruction risks was to engage in a strategy of peace, with arms control as an impor - tant pillar of such a strategy.

The Madrid Peace Conference (October 1991) was among the highlights of American strategic thinking after the Gulf War. It was part of the philosophy, advanced primarily by Secretary of State James Baker, that sought to translate and consolidate the victory of the American-led coalition in the Gulf into the establishment of a new regional coalition of peace. Multilater - alism was thought to be the prime modality to advance re - gional cooperation, to support and reinforce the traditional bilateral tracks. The Madrid framework gave birth to five mul- tilateral "working group" fora, one of which focuses on re gional security and arms control, known as Arms Control and Re - gional Security (ACRS) Working Group (the other four working groups were on water, economic cooperation and develop ment, the environment, and refugees).

While concerns over the nuclear issue led to the establishment of ACRS in 1991–93, this issue also led to the stalemate, impasse, and ultimate paralysis of ACRS in 1994–95. It is one thing to recognize the need to address the nuclear issue in the context of regional security and arms control, but it is another to address the issue in a substantial fashion. Thus far, the nuclear issue has failed to be opened to detailed discussion, let alone negotiation. The nuclear question is the single most problematic issue, and has not been integrated into the broader landscape of the "peace process" in the Middle East.

Why is this so? Can the nuclear question be incorporated into a meaningful agenda for the peace process and regional arms control? How, and under what political modalities? This chapter consists of two parts. The first, under the heading "problems," spells out the difficulties of future nuclear arms control in the Middle East. These problems make it difficult, if not impossible, to integrate the nuclear issue into the rest of the peace and arms control agenda. The second, under the heading "prospects," proposes and analyzes short- and long-term policy options on how to deal with the nuclear issue within the broader architecture of arms control and the peace process in the Middle East.

Problems

It is useful to look at several obstacles to meaningful pro - gress on nuclear arms control in the Middle East. There are two sets or types of problems.

The first set relates to obstacles intrinsic to the ACRS proc- ess, that is, problems regarding the relationship between the peace process and arms control, both on the substantive and formal levels. In this context, it is important to understand the historical evolution of the two seemingly irreconcilable ap - proaches that have characterized the way in which Egypt and Israel address the nuclear issue—"universal" versus "regional" approaches. After reviewing the ACRS record, the author sug- gests that at the heart of the current impasse in negotiations are the underlying problems of nuclear asymmetry and opac - ity. The second set of problems relates to WMD threats posed by states outside the peace process, particularly Iraq and Iran, whose nuclear programs undermine the entire regional arms control effort.

"Universalist" versus "Regional" Approaches

Negotiating regional security and arms control, especially nuclear arms control, is new to the states of the Middle East. Until 1992, there was no regional forum for negotiation and discussion of such issues. The context of the Arab-Israeli con flict did not permit its existence. The notion that Arab govern ments would sit with the Israeli leadership and discuss regional secu - rity and negotiate arms control agreements was for years un - thinkable to Arab states; it would have meant the *de facto* recognition of Israel, which was anathema to Arab governments.

This does not mean, of course, that the region's states have not issued declarations on general and nuclear disarmament before. In fact, Arab and Israeli diplomats have given endless speeches on disarmament over the years at the United Na - tions and other international fora. The general pattern since the 1970s has been for Arab states to call for regional nuclear disarmament and to point to Israel's refusal to sign the Nu - clear Nonproliferation Treaty (NPT), while Israel insisted on the establishment of peace as the prerequisite for negotiations on arms control and disarmament. The sole reason for these proclamations was to score points and counterpoints in the Arab-Israeli propaganda battle. Notwithstanding this pattern, all the states in the Middle East have signed and ratified the Partial Test Ban Treaty (PTBT) of 1963.

The most well-advertised disarmament idea that has circu - lated over the years, publicly endorsed by both Arabs and Israelis alike, is the establishment of a NWFZ in the Middle East. Iran and Egypt were the first to cosponsor such a reso - lution at the UN First Committee of the General Assembly in 1974. Resolution 9693 was unanimously adopted (128 votes with only two abstentions—Israel and Burma) on 9 December 1974. Since then the General Assembly has annually renewed Resolution 9693 with slight variations from year to year.[16]

During the 1970s, Israel abstained from voting either for or against the Iranian-Egyptian-sponsored resolution that had passed by an overwhelming majority. For the first time, how - ever, in 1980, Israel joined in supporting the NWFZ resolution at the United Nations. Thereafter, the resolution has been unanimously adopted each year without the need for a vote. Notably, all the Middle Eastern governments have expressed their support for the establishment of a NWFZ in their region.

This apparent regional consensus, however, has gone no - where and means very little since the prerequisites that each side has stipulated for its support of a regional NWFZ are patently unacceptable to the other. The Egyptian proposal stipulated, as a condition for the establishment of a NWFZ in the Middle East, that all parties adhere to the NPT. To high - light this point, Egypt ratified the NPT in early 1981, demon - strating its commitment to the idea of establishing a NWFZ even though Israel had not done so. For Egypt, the NPT/International Atomic Energy Agency (IAEA) safeguards regime was an indispensable mechanism for the establishment of a NWFZ in the region.[17] Avoiding the need for direct regional negotia - tions, the NPT approach meant that the nuclear issue would stand alone, isolated from all other matters of regional secu - rity and would require Israel to accept IAEA full-scope safe - guards on all its nuclear facilities.

While on the surface, the Egyptian proposal looked like a regional approach, it was in fact built on the NPT's universal mechanisms. Israel, which has refused to sign the NPT, em - phasized in its own NWFZ proposal the difference between the regional and the global, or universal, approaches to nonprolif - eration. The Israeli proposal called "upon all states in the Middle East and nonnuclear weapons states adjacent to the region . . . to convene at the earliest possible date a conference with a view to negotiating a multilateral treaty establishing a nuclear-weapons-free-zone in the Middle East."[18]

Israel proposed the NWFZ as a way to highlight its nonpro - liferation interests, despite its specific objections to the NPT. For Israel, a NWFZ is meant to be an alternative for NPT/IAEA mechanisms, which Israel considers deficient. It was a way for Israel to present a vision of its own of a peaceful Middle East free of nuclear weapons, while maintaining that there is an - other nonproliferation avenue—the regional one—besides the universalist NPT approach. For Israel, the terms and modali - ties of a Middle East NWFZ must be determined only through direct political and technical negotiations among all the re - gional parties, in relation to other regional security and arms control issues, and in direct reference to the overarching ques- tion of peaceful coexistence in the Middle East. [19] Behind the appearance of a regional consensus there persists a deadlock built upon opposing interests.[20]

In the pre-Persian Gulf War era, this difference of opinion over the NWFZ was politically immaterial. While both sides could claim the moral high ground, they knew that the entire exercise at the UN was futile. At best it presented different visions of the future; at worst, it was no more than a game of diplomatic posturing. Until the Arabs were ready to recognize Israel and negotiate with it on regional peace and security, the NWFZ proposal would remain purely theoretical. Israel, still a *de facto* nuclear power, had no difficulty in proposing a NWFZ, recognizing that nothing practical would be achieved by those diplomatic exercises in the absence of fundamental political change, while tacitly refusing to accept external restrictions on its freedom of action in the nuclear field. Certainly such a position was compatible with Israel's posture of nuclear opacity, and did not require any debate in Israel. For their part, the Arab states' attempt to link a NWFZ in the Middle East with the NPT was intended to embarrass Israel and to highlight its refusal to sign the NPT. The NWFZ impasse was thus convenient for the rhetoric of both sides. Israel emphasized the need for peace and regional security, and Arab leaders stressed Israel's refusal to sign the NPT.[21]

The ACRS Record: Hopes and Obstacles

The establishment of the ACRS working group in October 1991 as a multilateral forum was the direct result of Secretary of State James Baker's reading of the Middle East scene after the Gulf War. Baker designed the Madrid conference as a way to revive the Arab-Israeli peace process in the wake of the American-led victory in the Gulf. Baker envisioned the peace process to consist of two parallel tracks: (1) a bilateral track devoted to direct negotiations between Israel and its immediate Arab neighbors and (2) a multilateral track dedicated to promoting multilateral and regional issues that affect all states of the region. An interest in curbing proliferation of weapons of mass destruction was certainly considered an important shared concern.

ACRS was the highlight of Baker's two-track architecture of peace.[22] It meant the creation of a regional institution in which exchanges, discussions, and negotiations over all matters of regional security and arms control were possible. In a number of ways, ACRS appeared as a revolutionary departure from past Arab-Israeli exchanges. First, its very existence implied implicit recognition of Israel and its right to exist by all the

Arab members of ACRS. In this way, Israel's long-held insis - tence that direct negotiations were a condition for arms con - trol and disarmament was met by the very creation of ACRS. Second, it implied that ACRS members, the Arab states and Israel, shared certain security concerns, particularly regarding the proliferation of WMD, and hence accepted the notion of a regional forum to discuss common concerns of "regional secu - rity." Third, it implies a recognition that in the Middle East there exist "strategic asymmetries" that may defy the notion of "mutuality" in the context of the Arab-Israeli conflict. These asymmetries refer to issues such as population, territory, natural resources, and, of course, types of weaponry and mili- tary doctrine.

The establishment of ACRS meant an acceptance of the "regional" approach to arms control , but it also revealed its major shortcomings, especially the fundamental differences between Arab states (led by Egypt) and Israel about how to address the larger issues of arms control. These differences involved matters of both substance and form. By 1995—prior to and independent of the setbacks to the political peace proc- ess—it became evident that the ACRS forum was incapable of functioning as a substantive arms control mechanism. In fact, the ACRS process had broken down primarily due to major disagreements among the parties over the nuclear issue.

On the formal side, ACRS never became a truly regional forum. Although ACRS has included 14 Middle Eastern mem - ber states—including Egypt, Israel, Jordan, the Palestinian Authority, as well as members of the Gulf Cooperation Coun - cil, and some of the Arab Maghreb states—some of the most relevant states in the region are missing. Iraq, Iran, and Libya were not invited as parties to the ACRS (they also did not participate in the Madrid conference). Syria and Lebanon, while invited to the multilateral working groups, decided not to attend the multilateral meetings until they see significant progress in the bilateral peace talks with Israel. These absten- tions make it unlikely that any comprehensive agreements can soon be concluded through ACRS.

On the substantive side, it is evident that Arabs and Israelis have opposite interests, approaches, priorities, and agendas on matters of arms control, and in particular on the nuclear issue. These fundamental differences have surfaced in all the ACRS rounds held thus far. The apparent consensus on the long-term objectives of the process—the establishment of a zone free of all WMD—disguises the reality that these objectives are not likely to be translated into political action anytime soon. By 1995–96, in the wake of the Egyptian-Israeli confrontation over the issue of the NPT extension, it became evident that the ACRS process had reached a point of complete impasse.

The Underlying Issues: Asymmetry and Opacity

The impasse at ACRS is, to a large extent, due to the fundamentals of the nuclear issue in the Middle East. There is a vast asymmetry in nuclear capabilities between Israel and all the other states in the region. Such a fundamental asymmetry did not exist when the United States and the Soviet Union were conducting nuclear arms control negotiations in the 1960s; nor did it exist in the less structured and more rudimentary cases of nuclear rivalry between India and Pakistan or Argentina and Brazil.

Underlying this asymmetry (but hardly mentioned) is a basic divergence of interests and priorities between the parties to the ACRS. The Arab states, especially Egypt , seek to focus on the nuclear issue and to isolate it as much as possible from the rest of the security agenda. For Egypt, bringing an end to Israel's nuclear superiority is probably the single most important item on its national arms control agenda. It insists on entering into negotiations as early as possible, primarily through existing international treaties and organizations such as the NPT and the IAEA. [23] Egypt conceives of the establishment of a NWFZ through a predetermined and relatively autonomous time sequence, including both political declarations and activities on the ground.

Beyond the official Egyptian position, Egyptian analysts have repeatedly made the point that to discuss the establishment of a NWFZ, or WMDFZ in the Middle East, Israel must first ease its official policy of nuclear ambiguity and accept some measure of transparency for its nuclear capability. Some Egyptians have privately proposed that the timeline for establishing such a zone could be as long as 15 or 20 years, but insist that, in the end, "all Israeli nuclear weapons must be dismantled."[24]

Israelis, on the other hand, want to keep their nuclear monopoly indefinitely, or at least until regional peace is firmly established. They wish to keep their nuclear bargaining chip in play at least until the peace-making process is complete, insisting that the establishment of a NWFZ ought to be the last stage of arms control negotiations, linked to other issues of regional security and arms control. For Israel , the nuclear issue symbolizes the last stop on the arms control path; it is the strength that allows them to make territorial concessions.[25]

In general, Israel insists that the nuclear issue cannot be isolated from other elements of the arms control package, as the NPT would suggest, but that any discussion of further steps toward the establishment of a NWFZ must be linked with political progress on the peace front, as well as with progress in other areas of conventional and unconventional arms control. Israel has a clear edge and will want as many gains in peace and security as possible before it makes any concessions of its own on the nuclear issue.

This issue is compounded by Israel's long-standing policy of opacity and ambiguity regarding its nuclear capability, manifested by the three decades-old formula, "Israel will not be the first to introduce nuclear weapons to the Middle East." A certain transparency is required for any process of arms control, as evidenced by 30 years of arms control negotiations between the United States and the Soviet Union. To negotiate such agreements, the participants must know, and openly communicate, about what is on the table.

Opacity, or lack of transparency, makes it difficult for the parties to agree on the vocabulary that forms the basis of negotiations. For example, while the Arabs insist on a "full accounting of Israel's nuclear arsenal" as a necessary step for establishing a NWFZ, the current Israeli discourse does not allow discussion of Israeli "nuclear weapons." To "eliminate" or "dismantle" nuclear weapons, the weapons first need to be "introduced." Thus far, Israel claims not to have "introduced" them. The most that the Israeli nuclear discourse allows is to refer to an Israeli "nuclear option" as a "capability" consisting of "unsafeguarded nuclear facilities."

The present deadlock is likely to remain as long as both sides continue to stake too much on their declared long-term objectives regarding the establishment of a WMDFZ, especially on nuclear weapons. The substantive reason for this is known by all but openly acknowledged by none: until Israel feels secure in the new Middle East, it will continue to regard its unacknowledged nuclear deterrent as an essential ingredient for its national security. Many Israelis, especially on the left, believe that Israel's "nuclear option" has been significant in persuading Arab states to work toward peace. They believe that the way in which the Israeli bomb has manifested itself, both as a symbol and as a perception by the "Arab mindset," was an unspoken but important factor in Arab governments' acceptance of Israel's existence. Many Arab strategists, espe - cially Palestinians, half openly agree with this view. Therefore, it is the idea of a lasting peace that is at the heart of the Israeli proposal for a Middle East NWFZ.

Furthermore, as long as Iran, Iraq, and Syria are not among those meeting at the ACRS, it would be futile for Israel to start negotiating the establishment of a NWFZ in the Middle East. Without the presence of these and other relevant actors, there is no point in Israel discussing these highly complex matters. Israel made clear in the ACRS meetings that, as a matter of national strategy, it will continue to insist on linking progress on the nuclear issue with substantial political progress on the peace front, as well as on linking the nuclear issue to visible progress in other areas of arms control, both conventional and unconventional. Realistically, then, it should be clear that Is - rael will not hasten to establish a NWFZ anytime soon. On the contrary, Israeli defense sources have publicly insisted that a leaner peacetime Israeli army must have an even stronger strategic deterrent component. It is that component, specifi - cally its "nuclear option," that will preserve the peace.[26]

Though such views appear incompatible with the former Rabin government's visionary goals for the arms control proc - ess, including its support for the establishment of a NWFZ in the Middle East, this may not necessarily be true. [27] It means that as a practical reality, a NWFZ is not feasible for the near future. While it is important to set the long-term visionary goals for the arms control process, it should also be recognized that such a vision is only heuristic, not a blueprint for immediate action. The nuclear deadlock cannot be resolved by looking at the end result of the process—a NWFZ—but rather by break - ing the process down into smaller and more manageable issues.

Implicit in this point is a certain criticism of the mind-set that both Egypt and Israel bring to the nuclear issue. Egypt continues to overemphasize the nuclear issue, leading to the paralysis of the entire ACRS process. [28] Arab states must un- derstand and appreciate Israel's insistence on linkages be - tween the question of a NWFZ and the establishment of last - ing peace in the region. Trying to push the nuclear issue to the forefront would only reinforce Israeli steadfastness. As for Israel, much of its reluctance to allow nuclear arms control discourse is derived from its long-held commitment to the posture of nuclear opacity. By now this posture is more than a strategic posture; it is also a cultural and behavioral artifact intimately embedded in Israel's national security culture—in the values, attitudes, and norms passed on to those initiated into the culture. It is this culture which made the nuclear issue a paradigm of nuclear secrecy and taboo in Israel.

The culture of opacity is rooted in fundamental Israeli per - ceptions that developed over decades of Arab-Israeli conflict: nuclear weapons are vital to Israel's security; the Arabs should not be allowed to obtain these weapons; Israel should be al- lowed to keep a nuclear monopoly; nuclear issues must be kept out of normal public discourse; the issue should be left to anonymous nuclear professionals; and opacity has served Israel well and has no alternative. [29] Even in today's Israel, when all other security-related organizations and issues, in - cluding the Mossad and the General Security Service, have become a matter of public debate and criticism, the nuclear issue is conspicuous by its absence from the public agenda.[30]

For years, it was held that, despite the culture of opacity , Israeli leaders have adequately internalized the fundamental lessons of the nuclear age, that is, that nuclear weapons can- not be used short of the most extreme situations in which the existence and integrity of the state is in peril. Recently, how - ever, some credible Israeli analysts have expressed concerns that under the culture of opacity, present Israeli leadership may have developed a different attitude regarding nuclear weapons, namely that these weapons could be used even in situations that pose less than an existential threat to the state, and that they might be the "appropriate" Israeli re - sponse to an Iraqi chemical or biological attack. [31] If this is true, it is a chilling reminder of the dangers of opacity.

Long years of taboo and secrecy have resulted in a mind-set that resists the very theory and practice of arms control nego- tiations. Though there are hints of a readiness to rethink the issue, the burden of the past—the fear of the "slippery slope"—still dominates Israeli thinking on these sensitive mat- ters. Opacity—and official silence concerning even the policy itself—make it hard for outsiders to understand Israel's moti - vations. This results in a cycle of mutual distrust and disin - formation which undermines rather than increases Israel's security. If the arms control process requires educating one - self about the other's security needs and threat perceptions, Israel must explain why it first developed its "nuclear option" and why it must keep it until lasting peace arrives.

Outlyers: Iraq and Iran

Notwithstanding the problems of mindsets on the part of both Arabs and Israelis, the greatest obstacles to progress on the nuclear issue are those states which remain outside the ACRS process. The region's two most determined proliferators, Iran and Iraq, are not formal parties to the peace process , each for its own reasons. Consequently, they were not invited to the ACRS forum. Both have continued their pursuit of weap - ons of mass destruction. The lessons of the Gulf War— Hussein's fateful miscalculations in Kuwait, his devastating defeat in Desert Storm, Security Council Resolution 687, and subsequent revelations about the Iraqi nuclear program— must have reinforced both Iraqi and Iranian perceptions about nuclear weapons.

While Iraq is certainly more advanced in terms of research and development (R&D) and experience, it has been subject to the UNSCOM inspection and dismantling regime up until the end of 1998 when Iraq barred further inspections and created an impasse in the disarmament process. The Islamic Republic of Iran is a different matter. The Iranian proliferation effort, while certainly less advanced than that of Iraq, is no less of a political problem. Nuclear weapons have remained the ulti - mate symbol of political defiance, technological achievement, and deterrence vis-à-vis all of Iran's potential enemies. Unlike Iraq, Iran is not a defeated nation under an unprecedented Security Council/IAEA inspection regime, nor does it fall un - der UN trade sanctions. This makes it more difficult to trace incriminating evidence of NPT violations there. In addition, Iran's nuclear program is still in an early phase, at a stage where it is probably impossible to discern even the legal-con - ceptual difference between peaceful and nonpeaceful activi - ties. Compared to the Iraqi case after the passage of Security Council Resolution 687, the Iranian case offers neither techni- cal clarity nor legal and political mechanisms to obtain critical information.

Without focusing on the details of the WMD program of Iran and Iraq, a number of broader trends and lessons regarding the future of proliferation should be highlighted. First, the technologies for producing WMD and Scud-like delivery means are no longer cutting-edge technology. On the nuclear side, the basic technical knowledge to produce fissile material and to design simple nuclear weapons (fission-only) is now decades old; the consensus is that credible production of such weapons (with a Scud-like delivery system) needs no full-yield testing.[32] Given the current diffusion of technologies, informa - tion, and human resources, there is little doubt that a deter - mined state with sufficient resources could, in time, obtain access to nuclear weapons (and other WMD) technologies.

It has been commonly assumed that the production of fissi le material for nuclear weapons is a more difficult hurdle than weapons designed for would-be proliferators. During the first three decades of the nuclear age, the plutonium route was considered the preferable path to the bomb. This was a rather difficult and costly route that made efforts for long-term con - cealment virtually impossible. However, with the development of modern gas centrifuge machines in the 1960s, and the easier access to older separation technologies, the uranium route has become the preferred choice for clandestine prolif - erators for reasons that include access to technology, cheaper cost, and concealment.[33] Furthermore, much of the equipment needed for the uranium route is dual use by nature. It tends to lack distinctive characteristics, otherwise known as a "sig - nature," and this makes monitoring difficult.

Since mid-1991, Iraq's nuclear, biological, and chemical (NBC) weapons programs, as well as its ballistic missile pro - grams, have been meticulously studied by the United Nations Committee on Iraq and the IAEA, under the mandate of the UN Security Council Resolution 687 of 3 April 1991. While not all is yet known about Iraq's WMD programs , particularly in the biological field, some important general lessons can be drawn.[34] These lessons confirm suspicions concerning Iran's nuclear ambitions. [35]

To begin with, the Iraqi case shows how difficult it is to deny a determined proliferator state, especially one that is a signatory of the NPT. States with a limited industrial and technological base can obtain sufficient access to bomb-mak - ing technology and know-how to initiate a large-scale nuclear weapons program and can largely conceal it both from na - tional technical means of intelligence gathering and from the IAEA/ NPT safeguards regime. The IAEA/NPT safeguards were designed primarily to verify or to trace the diversion of de - clared assets; they were not designed as a mechanism to de - tect and reveal subversion or clandestine activities. This sug - gests that future clandestine nuclear weapons programs may develop to advanced stages before they are discovered.

The intelligence failure in the case of Iraq's nuclear program shows not only that major mistakes can be made in the allo - cation and evaluation of intelligence collection efforts, but also how profoundly imperfect is the entire enterprise of nuclear intelligence. Some of the most significant Iraqi nuclear facili - ties remained undiscovered long after UNSCOM had started its operations in Iraq; the first post-Gulf War discoveries were due largely to luck. The vast uncertainty regarding the North Korean bomb effort—questions whether plutonium has been pro-cessed thus far; if so, how much, and how advanced the North Koreans are in their weaponization work—is another stern reminder of the intrinsic limitations of nuclear intelligence.

In 1981 Israel successfully conducted a preemptive attack t o put an end to the Iraqi Osiraq reactor project . It was the first and only exercise of arms control by unilateral means, but it was a one-time shot. One of the clear lessons of the Gulf War was the uniqueness of the attack on Osiraq. It would be ex - tremely difficult to repeat such an operation in the future. Only UNSCOM, an arms denial regime backed by force, has been able to uncover much (but not all) of Iraq's nuclear program.

How can the nuclear issue be integrated into a framework of peace and regional security? How can this issue be incorpo - rated into the broader arms control process associated with the regional peace agenda? Thus far, the nuclear issue has proved to be the most sensitive and difficult element of all regional arms control matters. Notwithstanding this sensitiv - ity, the issue is essential for the arms control process, and certainly will not go away. Ideas on how to deal with this issue in a realistic way are badly needed.

Prospects

The second part of this chapter focuses on efforts to incor - porate the nuclear issue   within a regional architecture   of peace and arms control, as well as within the wider context of global nuclear disarmament.[36] It considers (1) an interim pro - posal (a fissile material cutoff agreement) to break the current impasse; and (2) such long-term ideas as a NWFZ and virtual nuclear arsenals for shaping the thinking on the nuclear issue within a framework of regional peace.

In Search of Interim Measures: The Fissile Material Cutoff Proposal

To recognize that the establishment of a NWFZ   , or more generally a WMDFZ, is a long-term objective—a visionary ob - jective that lies at the remote end of the arms control agenda meant to coincide with the end of the Arab-Israeli conflict— does not mean that the only alternative is to leave the nuclear issue untouched until the establishment of a lasting peace in the Middle East. For reasons encompassing the peace process and (to a lesser degree) global nonproliferation interests, it is evident that the nuclear issue in the Middle East, including Israel's nuclear capability, must be addressed. In particular, some interim nuclear arms control measures can and should be discussed.[37]

One idea which might be both constructive and feasible is the proposal to halt the production of fissile material for nuclear weapons, commonly known as the cutoff proposal. The appeal of a Fissile Material Cutoff Treaty (FMCT) lies in the apparent simplicity and intuitiveness of the underlying idea: since nuclear weapons are made of a few kilograms of fissile material—either plutonium (Pu) or highly enriched uranium (HEU)—a verifiable prohibition on the unsafeguarded production of these materials would disallow production of new nuclear weapons; hence, it would impose a ceiling on the possible number of nuclear weapons. Since a treaty obligation to ban the production of fissile material must be verifiable, all signatory states would have to accept international (presumably IAEA) safeguards on all their nuclear facilities—past, present, and future—to verify that no weapons-usable fissile materials were being produced. Such a treaty would not preclude the production of fissile materials by its signatories for such purposes other than weapons as reactor grade plutonium or low-enriched uranium (LEU) and under safeguards. Furthermore, no other nuclear weapons-related activities, other than the production of new fissile material, would be affected by the FMCT; these activities would remain outside of safeguards.[38]

Since the cutoff proposal would put no additional legal constraints on nonnuclear weapons states (NNWS) which are already parties to the NPT— (Article III states that NNWS must place all their nuclear materials under IAEA full-scope safeguards)—the countries directly affected by the cutoff are the five declared nuclear weapons states (NWS) and, most significantly, the three de facto NWS states outside the NPT: India, Israel, and Pakistan. Indeed, much of the motivation for the cutoff proposal is precisely to bring these three states into alignment with the nonproliferation regime. In effect, the undeclared nuclear weapon states would accept a capping or freezing of their fissile material production programs in return for grandfathering their current, unsafeguarded stockpiles.

In May 1991, in the wake of the Gulf War and the imposition of UN Security Council Resolution 687 on Iraq, the Bush administration proposed its own arms control initiative for the

Middle East. One element of the initiative was a proposal prohibiting the production of fissile material as a necessary step toward the establishment of a Middle East nuclear-weapon-free zone. The Middle East arms control initiative "call[ed] on regional states to implement a verifiable ban on the production and acquisition of weapons-usable nuclear material (enriched uranium and separated plutonium)."[39] This was the first American proposal that dealt with the nuclear reality of the Middle East, beyond proforma support for the NPT. The Bush initiative, however, was no more than a loose set of ideas for possible future arms control arrangements in the Middle East, and resulted in a decision not to press the question of fissile material production pending further pro - gress on the peace front and to work within the newly estab - lished ACRS forum. Since then the United States, as the co-chair of the ACRS talks, has failed to place the cutoff issue on the ACRS agenda, fearing it would be premature.

The introduction of a fissile material cutoff proposal may be among the most meaningful interim arms control measures that could break the present Arab-Israeli impasse over the nuclear issue. In the appropriate political context, it may even be the most attractive proposal since it seems to offer both sides new and significant benefits, while also leaving their concerns open for further discussion later in the process.

From an Israeli perspective, a properly-written cutoff agree-ment could provide a number of advantages. First, it could lend a certain legitimacy to Israel's existing stockpile of weap - ons-grade fissile material; in a sense, the cutoff proposal im - plicitly legitimizes Israel's nuclear status. Second, a cutoff pro-posal commits signatories to frank discussions about "fissile material," without referring in any way to actual weapons or even to previous production of weapons-grade material. This implies that the cutoff proposal could allow Israel to maintain at least some elements of its policy of opacity and ambiguity. Third, and perhaps most significantly, the introduction of a fissile material cutoff would probably loosen the foundations of opacity. It is extremely unlikely that a discussion of such a far-reaching idea could be conducted in total secrecy without public feedback. Israelis should recognize that what is at stake is too important to be left to a handful of ministers and anonymous bureaucrats. Public discourse concerning a cutoff treaty would inevitably force Israel to move to a post-opacity phase. Thus, a FMCT would increase both the legitimacy and the transparency of Israel's nuclear program.

A cutoff arrangement could serve the Arabs states' interests as well. Even if it allowed some remnants of opacity to persist, it would still cap Israel's unsafeguarded nuclear program. In - deed, it would freeze Israel's production of fissile material and, by implication, impose quantitative constraints on Israel's nu- clear capabilities. This would obviously do much to meet the Arabs governments' goal of curtailing the Israeli nuclear arsenal.

Political Conditions for Interim Measures

Only within the context of a comprehensive peace agree - ment with Syria, including a substantial mutual security and arms control package, might Israel agree to consider a nuclear component to the peace treaty. Such a component would per- haps be in the form of a joint Syrian-Israeli declaration de - nouncing all WMD, which could be presented as a first step toward the establishment of a Middle East WMDFZ. Any Israeli pledges in the area of WMD and their delivery means would have to be reciprocated by similar undertakings by Syria that also in cluded demilitarization in the conventional field. Notwith - standing the strategic issues involved, it would be domestically difficult for any Israeli government to appear to make conces - sions on the territorial and nuclear fronts simultaneously.[40]

However, if any interim nuclear arrangement is possible for the Middle East, the cutoff proposal seems the most likely because it embraces the two most important features of Is - rael's policy of nuclear opacity: it is a future-oriented bargain, explicitly ignoring the past while implicitly acknowledging its reality; and it makes no generic or specific reference to nu clear weapons as such, only banning fissile material for weapons. In the past, nuclear opacity in the Middle East has been a sub - stitute for discussion and negotiation, but it need not be that way in the future. Just as opacity helped to create construc - tive ambiguity in the past, it could also contribute to creating constructive ambiguities for both security and arms control in the future.

The Long-Term Vision: The Virtue of Virtual Weapons

What should be the ultimate vision of the arms control discussion? On one level, the answer is simple and straight - forward. All parties of the ACRS forum have publicly agreed that the visionary objective of the arms control process is a peaceful Middle East free of all weapons of mass destruc - tion—that is, free of NBC weapons. Since 1990, when Iraq threatened Israel with the use of chemical weapons, Egypt has stated that all three types of weapons of mass destruction are intimately linked to one another and, therefore, must be banned in toto from the Middle East. Furthermore, Cairo has made the point that it would be impossible to establish re - gional peace without ridding the region of all weapons of mass destruction, including Israel's nuclear weapons.

While Israel has vehemently refused to discuss the nuclear issue in substance at the ACRS forum, arguing that political conditions in the region do not allow them to address the nuclear issue, it has never disputed the common vision of a peaceful Middle East free of weapons of mass destruction. [41] On the contrary, all Israeli governments, Likud (Shamir) and Labor (Rabin, Peres) alike, have been on record supporting the proposition that after the establishment of a regional peace, Israel would be ready to enter into substantial negotiations on establishing a WMDFZ in the Middle East. In pledging this, Israeli leaders seem to have accepted the principle of equality and nondiscrimination regarding WMD, where a peaceful Mid - dle East must be free of all nuclear weapons. [42] Put another way, no country in the Middle East should have the right to possess weapons of mass destruction after a negotiated peace.

Israeli political leaders and the public at large, however, seem to disagree with such diplomatic formulations. Without openly challenging Israel's stance on NWFZ and WMDFZ, coa - lition and opposition leaders seem to agree that, even in the event of a formal peace, Israel should not give up its nuclear option. Former Prime Minister Benyamin Netanyahu in 1996 clarified the Israeli position by noting that "lasting peace" could only mean peace among democracies: until the region becomes democratic, Israel is forced to maintain its strategic deterrence. [43] Similarly, present Prime Minister Ehud Barak , the leader of the Labor party, stated that Israel would need to maintain its nuclear option indefinitely. Netanyahu and Barak seem to agree that the nuclear option constitutes the foundation upon which regional peace rests. The peace itself is based on the presence of Israeli nuclear weapons.

The view that there can be no peace without an Israeli nuclear deterrent stems, in part, from the conviction that Israel's nuclear option has been a significant factor in persuading the Arab world to accept Israel and to make peace with it. Recent polls indicate that this view is overwhelmingly supported by the Israeli public. [44] Nearly all Israelis consider the nuclear option indispensable to their security, a view that will not completely recede once a comprehensive peace treaty is signed. After all, a regional peace treaty that formally ends the Arab-Israeli conflict would not change Israel's fundamental geopolitical predicament. Israel would still see itself as a small Jewish island surrounded by a vast Arab sea. The holocaust's impact on the Israeli national psyche would not disappear, and Israel's nuclear deterrent capability would remain as a hedge against possible future hostilities.

Until the 1990s, this tension between the two Israeli positions regarding the future of Israel's nuclear capability was hardly visible. To the extent that it was recognized, it was politically immaterial. As long as the Arab-Israeli conflict continued, in most respects unabated, talk of a link between peace and the nuclear issue was academic. This was another great advantage of opacity: it enforced a lack of conceptual clarity about Israel's long-term intentions and obscured the contradiction between Israel's commitment to acquire and preserve a nuclear weapons capability and its commitment not to nuclearize the Middle East. Under opacity, Israel has been able to project opposing objectives without having to explain.

The nuclear impasse in ACRS is not only about procedures, timetables or political posturing. It also concerns the future and legitimacy of Israel's nuclear deterrent. Would Israel really be willing to trade its nuclear option for peace? What does it mean for Israel to accept a verifiable NWFZ? Could Israel still maintain elements of a nuclear deterrent even under a NWFZ?

The idea of "nuclear virtuality" or a "virtual nuclear arsenal," a phrase that only recently has entered the lexicon of nuclear strategy, arms control, and nonproliferation, could provide the key to addressing these questions. [45] In virtual parlance, nu - clear arsenals are discussed not in terms of the physical hardware of nuclear weapons, but rather in terms of the knowledge and experience required to design, test, assemble, and deploy the arsenal. When the know-how concerning the requirements to produce nuclear weapons is widespread, virtual arsenals become a reality that cannot be ignored.

Of primary importance to understanding the notion of vir - tual nuclear arsenals are the concepts of knowledge and experience, concepts that have been systematically neglected by the arms control community practically since the 1946 Acheson-Lilienthal report. The IAEA/NPT system of declara - tions and inspections was designed exclusively to reveal the diversion of nuclear material from civilian to military uses— the primary concern at the time the NPT was negotiated. The framers of the NPT recognized that knowledge and experience cannot be subjected to effective international control and safe- guards, and international control of nuclear-related research cannot be effectively enforced without severe infringement on the principles of scientific freedom and national sovereignty. Other proposed nuclear arms agreements, such as the Com - prehensive Test Ban Treaty (CTBT) and the FMCT, also deal only with the physical aspects of nuclear weapons. But it is exactly these nonphysical aspects of nuclear weapons that could, in principle, give states the confidence to accept the military and political risks associated with disarmament.

It appears that legally there is a vast gray area concerning what a nation is entitled to retain under the NPT after it has dismantled its nuclear weapons hardware. Would retaining a small R&D—but not a production—program constitute a viola- tion of Article II of the NPT? This is unclear. What about main- taining a modest stewardship program to retain a full record of the program's past technical accomplishments? A stewardship program would hardly seem to violate any explicit NPT obliga - tions, which are, after all, future-oriented; but would it violate the spirit of the NPT pledge? Again, this is unclear. These ambiguities highlight the virtues of the NWFZ over the NPT as a normative approach to denuclearization: while the NPT is vague and ambiguous on matters of rolling-back, a NWFZ treaty need not be; negotiations could be conducted so as to incorporate specific state and regional concerns.

While controlling, safeguarding and dismantling such physical entities as warheads, nuclear material, and facilities is, in principle, a straightforward matter, this is not the case with the dismantling of nuclear weapons knowledge and experience stored in the human mind and embodied in coherent organizational structures. Such a commodity is closely tied to the trial-and-error process characteristic of human thinking as well as aspects of human organization. Even if all the physical carriers of that knowledge (e.g., technical reports, photos, tapes, or discs) were destroyed, as long as there remained a cadre of scientists and engineers experienced in the development and production of atomic weapons, it could all be easily done again, certainly faster than the first time.

Virtual nuclear weapons capabilities are, to some degree, already a reality of physics. Virtual arsenals might allow states to renounce ready-to-go, assembled nuclear weapons, while keeping some elements of nuclear deterrence in place. The potential value of virtual weapons is for states that have decided to reduce or eliminate their nuclear arsenals and wish to avoid any residual risks of doing so. Israel, especially if it enters into significant interim nuclear confidence building, could view nurturing and strengthening virtual capabilities as critical prerequisites for disarming while ensuring security.

Concluding Thoughts

The future of nuclear arms control in the Middle East depends primarily on two broader regional developments: progress toward the settlement of the Arab-Israeli conflict; and political, social, and technological developments in states outside the peace process. It is evident that without addressing these two issues—placing the peace process in motion again and stemming the proliferation ambitions of Iraq and Iran—there is little chance for progress on the nuclear question. However, these two issues are not unrelated. Effort towards resolving the Arab-Israeli conflict, associated with a meaningful arms control process, is probably the most promising long-term strategy to contain the threats from Iraq and Iran.

Furthermore, substantive discussion of the nuclear issue is essential and should not be put aside until everything else is settled. Both sides need to alter their basic approaches, which stem largely from fixed and obsolete mind-sets. The Arab states' ongoing insistence that Israel declare, safeguard, and finally dismantle its nuclear capability as a condition to re - gional peace is untenable and counterproductive. Egypt's per - sistence, in particular, is self-defeating. Pushing Israel into a corner on this highly sensitive issue only disrupts the arms control process. The nuclear question cannot be isolated from the rest of the regional security agenda, including other WMD matters and issues of restructuring conventional forces in the region. Arms control initiatives must recognize the fundamen - tal asymmetry between Israel and Arab strategic capabilities.

Israel's position is misguided as well. To legitimize its right to a nuclear arsenal as an insurance policy, Israel must be ready to explain the rationale for its nuclear option and, ulti - mately, to resolve the apparent tension between its desire to maintain a future nuclear option and its own visionary goals of a WMDFZ for arms control. Only then can Israel solidify a national strategy for nuclear arms control negotiations. A self-confident Israel can and should find ways under which the nuclear issue could be addressed, primarily on an interim and unilateral basis, without compromising its existential security and its ultimate insurance policy. Only if both sides make profound changes in their mindsets and resulting strategies can they begin to take initial steps towards controlling weap - ons of mass destruction in the Middle East.

Notes

1. Since 1955 David Ben Gurion was aware, and concerned, of the existence of an Egyptian chemical weapons capability. At about this time he apparently ordered that Israel beef up its own program. Aluf Benn, "The Project that Preceded the Nuclear Option" (in Hebrew), *Ha'aretz*, 2 March 1955. A veiled reference to Gurion's order can be found in Munya Mardor, *Rafael* (Tel Aviv: Ministry of Defense, 1981), 128. According to Mardor, "Ben Gurion followed the progress of the project, asking detailed questions, evidently concerned that we would meet the deadline he set, worrying that the enemy would have such a capability and we would have nothing to retaliate or deter."

2. For a comprehensive narrative, see Avner Cohen, *Israel and the Bomb* (New York: Columbia University Press, 1998).

3. Avner Cohen, "Cairo, Dimona and the June 1967 War," *The Middle East Journal* 50, no. 2 (Spring 1996): 190–210. Cohen, *Israel and the Bomb*, chap. 13.

4. Cohen, *Israel and the Bomb*, chap. 14.

5. For the story of how Israel made the decision to attack Osiraq, see Shlomo Nakdimon, *First Strike: The Exclusive Story of how Israel Foiled Iraq's Attempt to get the Bomb* (New York: Summit Books, 1987).

6. Cohen, "The Lessons of Osiraq and the American Counterproliferation Debate," in *International Perspectives on Counterproliferation,* eds. Mitchell Reiss and Harald Muller, Working Paper No. 99 (Washington, D.C.: The Woodrow Wilson Center for International Studies, January 1995), 73–102.

7. On the Iraqi-Israeli dialogue on nuclear weapons in the period that preceded the Gulf War, see Cohen and Marvin Miller, "Nuclear Shadows in the Middle East: Prospects for Arms Control in the Wake of the Gulf Crisis," *Security Studies* 1, no. 1 (Autumn 1991): 54–77; also Amatzia Baram, "Iraqi Imagery of Non-Conventional Deterrence vis-à-vis Israel and its Application in the Gulf War," unpublished manuscript; and Amatzia Baram, "Israeli Deterrence, Iraqi Responses," *Orbis* 36, no. 3 (Summer 1992): 397–409.

8. Egyptian Deputy Prime Minister and Minister of Foreign Affairs to the UN Secretary General, letter, subject: the Mubarak Initiative, 16 April 1990, cited in Shai Feldman, *Nuclear Weapons and Arms Control in the Middle East* (Cambridge, Mass.: CSIA/MIT Press, 1997), 297.

9. UN Security Council Resolution 687 was passed on 3 April 1991. Two subsequent resolutions, 707 (passed on 15 August 1991) and 715 (passed on 15 October 1991), reaffirmed and extended the provisions of 687.

10. Avner Cohen and Marvin Miller, "Iraq and the Rules of the Nuclear Game," *The Bulletin of Atomic Scientists,* July–August 1991, 10–11, 44.

11. The White House, "Fact Sheet on Middle East Arms Control Initiative," 29 May 1991. For excerpts, see Shai Feldman, 303–4.

12. It appears that such sentiments had already played a role in Anwar al-Sadat's thinking that led to his groundbreaking trip to Jerusalem. Ezer Weizman, the president of Israel and defense minister during the Camp David peace negotiations with Egypt, repeatedly remarked that on his first night in Israel, President Sadat invoked Israel's nuclear capability as one of the primary reasons for his decision to make peace with Israel. Ezer Weizman, *The War Over Peace* (in Hebrew) (Tel Aviv: Edanim, 1981), 85–87. President Weizman emphasized this point in many conversations with the author, which Mr. Mustafa Halil, the Prime Minister of Egypt under Sadat, confirmed in a conversation with the author (Cairo, June 1990).

13. While Israel sees itself as the first nation to use nondiplomatic means to counter hostile proliferation—Israel's precursor to its "counterproliferation" doctrine—cooperation in this regard with other states, particularly the United States, has now become a necessity. Yitzhak Rabin, "Only the US Can Prevent Proliferation" (in Hebrew), *Davar*, 17 January

1992; Ze'ev Schiff, "Race Against Time" (in Hebrew), *Politika*, March 1992, 14–17.

14. Indeed, the most recent crisis with Iraq highlights these symbolic and concrete issues concerning the use of weapons of mass destruction in the Middle East. Israel's panicked reaction to the very remote eventuality that it might be attacked by Iraqi chemical or biological weapons, and the suggestions that Israel might respond with the use of nuclear weapons, is a case in point.

15. This was very apparent in Rabin's inaugural address to the Knesset on 13 July 1992, when he stated, "Already in its initial stages, the Government, possibly with the cooperation of other countries, will give its attention to the foiling of every possibility that any of Israel's enemies would get hold of nuclear weapons." See also his article, "Taking Advantage of the Time-Out" (in Hebrew), *Politika*, March 1992, 28–29.

16. For a detailed history of the Iranian-Egyptian NWFZ proposal, see Mahmoud Karem, *A Nuclear Weapon-Free-Zone in the Middle East: Problems and Prospects* (New York: Greenwood Press, 1988), 91–117. Karem made the point that the Iranian-Egyptian proposal was born in response to the reports that Israel armed nuclear weapons during the 1973 war. See also the UN report to the Secretary General, *Establishment of a Nuclear Weapon-Free Zone in the Region of the Middle East,* A/45/435 (New York: United Nations, 10 October 1990), 6–7.

17. See also Lawrence Scheinman, "Modalities for Verifying a Middle East Nuclear Weapons Free Zone, Practical Peacemaking in the Middle East," in *Arms Control and Regional Security,* ed. by Steven Spiegel and David Pervan (New York: Garland Publishing Co., 1995).

18. UN General Assembly, 35th sess., First Committee, "Establishment of a Nuclear-Weapon-Free-Zone in the Region of the Middle East—Israel: Draft Resolution," agenda item no. 38, 31 October 1980.

19. Shalheveth Freier, the former director-general of the Israeli Atomic Energy Commission and subsequently a member of the Israeli delegation to the First Committee, is one of the Israelis who articulated this vision. Freier, "A Nuclear-Weapons-Free-Zone in the Middle East and its Ambiance," unpublished manuscript, Wiezmann Institute, Rehovot, Israel, 1993.

20. On this impasse see UN General Assembly, "Establishment of a Nuclear-Weapon-Free-Zone in the Region of the Middle East," 23–25.

21. Ibid.

22. For a comprehensive historical review of the ACRS process, see Bruce Jentleson, "The Middle East Arms Control and Regional Security (ACRS) Talks: Progress, Problems, and Prospects," Policy Paper no. 26, Institute on Global Conflict and Cooperation, 1996; Peter Jones, "Arms Control in the Middle East: Some Reflections on ACRS," *Security Dialogue* 28, no. 1 (1997): 57–70; Joel Peters, *Pathways to Peace: The Multilateral Arab-Israeli Peace Talks* (London: Royal Institute of International Affairs, 1996).

23. The Egyptian stance was strongly expressed by the Egyptian foreign minister, Amre Mussa, during his visit to Israel in early September. Mussa urged Israel to sign the NPT and dismantle its nuclear capability. He also suggested that Egypt would not sign the Chemical Weapons Convention (CWC) if Israel continues to remain outside the NPT See *Ha'aretz*, 31 August, and 1 September 1994.

24. This is based on private communications with Egyptian specialists, mostly senior diplomats and academics, at various meetings during 1997–1998. On this issue, see also Shai Feldman, "Israel," in *Nuclear Proliferation After the Cold War*, eds. Mitchell Reiss and Robert S. Litwak (Washington, D.C.: Woodrow Wilson Center Press, 1994), 80–82; Ze'ev Schiff, "What Are The Arabs Afraid Of?" (in Hebrew), *Ha'aretz*, 26 June 1991.

25. This kind of posturing was already evident during the first two rounds of the bilateral talks on arms control in Moscow in January 1992 and in the Washington "seminar" in May 1992. See Ruth Sinai, "Mideast Arms Talks," *Associated Press*, 11 May 1992.

26. Aluf Benn, "When Lasting Peace Comes" (in Hebrew), *Ha'aretz*, 29 September 1993.

27. Israel presented its "visionary goals" for the arms control agenda in a speech by Foreign Minister Shimon Peres on the occasion of the signing of the CWC. The text was released in a statement by the Foreign Ministry, Jerusalem, 14 January 1993.

28. Steven Greenhouse, "Israelis Offering to Leave Golan, Negotiators Say," *New York Times*, 18 May 1994.

29. In *Israel and the Bomb*, I analyze the emergence of this culture of opacity in Israeli society.

30. The sensitivity is evident in the fact that there exists hardly any substantive academic literature on this subject. In Israel, the only nation in the region known to possess a nuclear capability, scholars and analysts feel inhibited to address this issue, and even more so to criticize opacity.

31. Such concerns led Israeli analyst Ze'ev Schiff to propose a law that would place checks and balances on Israel's decision-making system in this most sensitive field. Ze'ev Schiff, "The Red Button Law" (in Hebrew), *Ha'aretz*, 13 March 1998 (translation in Ha'aretz's English Web Page, http://www.haaretz.co.il/eng/htmls/). See also Nahum Barnea and Shimon Shipper, "The Button and the Finger" (in Hebrew), *Yediot Ahronot*, 27 February 1998; cf. Ze'ev Schiff, "With a Finger on the Trigger" (in Hebrew), *Ha'aretz*, 13 February 1998.

32. Marvin Miller, "Weapons of Mass Destruction and Advanced Delivery Systems in the Middle East," in *Powder Keg in the Middle East*, eds. Geoffrey Kemp and Janice Gross Stein (Lanham, Md.: Rowman & Littlefield, 1995), 250. Miller maintains that even access to more advanced nuclear weapons, included those that are based on the principle of fusion (boosted and thermonuclear weapons), is more available now than ever before. While the consensus in the weapons community is that such advanced weapons

require testing, Miller points out that "if it is not essential to minimize the weapon's size and weight and to predict its yield precisely, computational power well below the level available in today's personal computers should suffice to develop weapons at all levels of technical sophistication, including fission-fusion bombs, with only a minimal number of such full-scale tests."

33. Ibid., 250–55.

34. Judith Miller, "Baghdad Arrests a Germ Specialist," *New York Times,* 24 March 1998, A1; William J. Broad and Judith Miller, "Iraq's Deadliest Arms: Puzzles Breed Fears," *New York Times,* 26 February 1998, A1, A10–11; Richard Spertzel, "Iraq's Biological Warfare Program: Past, Present and Future Challenges," *Policywatch,* 6 February 1998.

35. For a comprehensive reconstruction of Iraq's nuclear program, based on UNSCOM inspections in the period 1991–1996, see David Albright, Frans Berkhout, and William Walker, *Plutonium and Highly Enriched Uranium 1996: World Inventories, Capabilities and Policies* (London: SIPRI/Oxford University Press, 1997), 309–50. For a list of the UN documents on Iraq's nuclear program, see Albright, Berkhout, and Walker, 310, footnote 2. For an updated assessment on Iraq's nuclear weapons program, see David Albright, "Iraq's Nuclear Weapons Programs: Assessing the Issues in 1998," edited transcript of remarks given at the Washington Institute for Near East Policy on 23 January 1998.

36. A forthcoming book by the author reviews the new global environment regarding nuclear weapons. To think about the nuclear future of the Middle East, other visions of the future of nuclear weapons are considered and analyzed. The author examines a number of different visions of the future of nuclear weapons held by states that have developed nuclear weapons. These nuclear designs are exemplified in the views of the five de jure members of the nuclear club, as well as in the cases of South Africa and Latin America (Brazil and Argentina).

37. This is also the general approach of the 1990 UN report, *Establishment of a Nuclear Weapon-Free Zone in the Region of the Middle East,* 30–47.

38. Frans Berkhout et al., "A Cutoff in the Production of Fissile Material," *International Security* 19, no. 3 (Winter 1994/95): 4; Savita Pande, *Fissile Material for Nuclear Weapons,* Occasional Paper Series (New Delhi: Institute for Defence Studies and Analyses, December 1997); Frank von Hippel, "The Fissile Cutoff: Is There a Way Forward?" unpublished paper presented at the conference on The Future of Nuclear Weapons: A US-India Dialogue, 5–8 May 1997; Annette Schaper, *A Treaty on the Cutoff of Fissile Material for Nuclear Weapons—What to Cover? How to Verify?* (Frankfurt: Peace Research Institute, Frankfurt Reports no. 48, July 1997); Stefan Keller, "Some Striking Similarities and Some Telling Dissimilarities Between a Cutoff Convention and a CTBT," in Schaper, 56–69.

39. White House Fact Sheet on the Middle East Arms Control Initiative, 29 May 1991; see also Avner Cohen and Marvin Miller, "Defusing the Nuclear Mideast," *New York Times,* 30 May 1991.

40. Israel may feel less secure in the immediate period after trading land for peace, leading some to argue that a nuclear deterrent is the ultimate guarantee of a smaller Israel.

41. This way of thinking was manifest in the language of the Israeli-Jordanian peace treaty, where the two parties took upon themselves the commitment "to work, as a matter of priority and as soon as possible in the context of the ACRS towards the creation of a Middle East free from weapons of mass destruction, both conventional and non-conventional, in the context of comprehensive, lasting and stable peace, characterized by the renunciation of the use of force, reconciliation and good will." The Israel-Jordan Peace Treaty, Article 4, 7, b. The English text appeared in the *New York Times,* 27 October 1994.

42. Shimon Peres, the Israeli leader who made Israel's nuclear option a reality, expressed this recognition in the most explicit and straightforward way. In December 1995 he made headlines worldwide when he responded to a question about Israel's nuclear future by saying, "Give me peace, and we'll give up the nuclear program." Serge Schmeman, "Peres Says Israel, with Regional Pact, Would End Atom Effort," *New York Times,* 23 December 1995.

43. Netanyahu made the point in his first speech before the US Congress, shortly after his election in 1996. A similar point was made by Gideon Frank, the director-general of the Israeli Atomic Energy Commission, at an ISIS seminar at the Shalheveth Freier Center for Peace, Science and Technology, Nahal Soreq Nuclear Research Center, 16 May 1996.

44. Alan Arian, *Security Threatened: Surveying Israeli Opinion on Peace and War* (New York: Cambridge University Press, 1995).

45. Michael J. Mazarr, ed., *Nuclear Weapons in a Transformed World: The Challenge of Virtual Nuclear Arsenals* (New York: St. Martin's Press, 1997); Avner Cohen and Joseph Pilat, "Assessing Virtual Nuclear Arsenals," *Survival* 40, no. 1 (Winter 1998): 129–44.

Chapter 5

The Egyptian-Israeli Confrontation over the Nuclear Nonproliferation Treaty

W. Andrew Terrill

Egyptian regional policy has often been a vital factor influ - encing Arab-Israeli peace efforts. Under the Mubarak govern - ment, Egypt retains a strong vested interest in a successful peace process which addresses fundamental Arab interests on the Palestinian issue, the future disposition of the Golan Heights, and also on various multilateral issues including nuclear non- proliferation and arms control.[1] A successful peace process that meets key Arab concerns will vindicate Egypt's decision to become the first Arab nation to establish full diplomatic rela - tions with Israel. Such success will also help to dispel Arab nationalist concerns about Cairo's close ties to the United States and perhaps help to marginalize violent, antiregime, Islamic radicals struggling against the Mubarak government.[2]

The Egyptians consistently describe their support for the peace process as requiring it to serve the best interests of the Arabs. They suggest that Egypt is prepared to act assertively and accept tension in US-Egyptian relations to advance Arab concerns. Cairo's hesitancy about real and perceived conces - sions to Israel is therefore directly related to President Hosni Mubarak's efforts to appear as the leading defender of Arab interests.[3] The president deeply cherishes his reputation as a sophisticated international leader and thus cannot appear un- able to cope with Israeli or US diplomacy.

Egypt has played the role of the leading defender of Arab rights in a variety of ways such as using its relations with both the United States and Israel to intercede for a variety of Arab actors in political conflict with those states. Additionally, the Mubarak government has strongly challenged the Israeli deci- sion to remain a nontreaty party to the Nuclear Nonprolifera - tion Treaty (NPT). Cairo views the application of a major global arms control treaty to all regional states, except Israel, as an unacceptable double standard imposed upon Arab nations. Unfortunately, this Egyptian priority touches on a fundamen -

tal and, currently, nonnegotiable Israeli security concern. The Israelis have shown no interest in serious discussions of their own nuclear capabilities and are especially reluctant to do so under Arab pressure.

Egyptian-Israeli disagreement over nuclear arms control presented a major complication for the peace process even prior to the May 1996 election of hard-line Israeli prime minister Benyamin Netanyahu. This conflict has also been espe - cially troubling for efforts to obtain even limited arms control measures usually described as confidence and security build - ing measures (CSBM).[4] Cairo's absolute disagreement with Is - rael's decision to remain outside of the NPT has also resulted in an Egyptian-led diplomatic offensive against the Israeli nu - clear weapons option. The ultimate goal of this effort has been to pressure Israel into joining the NPT as a nonnuclear weap - ons power. As such, Israel would be required to destroy any existing nuclear weapons and place its nuclear facilities under international safeguards. Such an outcome is anathema to the Israelis who view Egyptian policies as utterly unreasonable. Additionally, the diplomatic struggle over this issue has ampli fied and complicated other Egyptian-Israeli differences.

Egypt's Changing Approach to the Israeli Nuclear Issue

Egypt's 1990s diplomatic offensive is only Cairo's most re - cent effort to respond to Israeli nuclear activities. The Arab debate regarding Israel's nuclear weapons potential first emerged in December 1960 following Western press reports announcing the existence of a nuclear reactor in southern Israel near the city of Dimona. Initially, the Arab states were unwilling to accept the possibility that Israel might be engaged in serious nuclear weapons progress, and they treated this information with great skepticism. Key Egyptian leaders, in - cluding President Gamel Abdel Nasser , seem to have viewed Israeli nuclear activities as a bluff or intimidation tactic rather than a serious effort to build indigenous nuclear weapons. Cairo was especially reluctant to admit that Israel was moving ahead in such a complex and vital field as nuclear technology while Egypt was doing nothing in this discipline. This process of denial was clearly apparent in the Arab and especially the Egyptian media at the time[5]

Throughout the 1960s the Egyptian media and leadership continued to express strong doubts about Israel's ability to build nuclear weapons. While Egyptian leaders did acknow - ledge that Israel might be conducting nuclear weapons re - search, both Presidents Nasser and Anwar Sadat also publicly claimed that reports of finished or near-finished Israeli nu - clear weapons were either false rumors or more probably Is - raeli psychological warfare.[6] In the early 1960s President Nas- ser even promised swift preemptive military action if Israel actually began making serious progress on nuclear weapons.[7] Yet, in contrast to these public Egyptian doubts, Israeli scholar Avner Cohen maintains that Israel had its first two operational nuclear weapons by the time of the June 1967 war. French journalist Pierre Pean also stated in his book *Les Deux Bombs,* that the Israelis had completed at least one bomb by 1966.[8]

It also seems clear that Egyptian leaders became more con - cerned about the existence of Israeli nuclear weapons in the era between the 1967 and 1973 wars. These leaders chose to downplay their concerns because of ongoing preparations for the conventional war with Israel that was ultimately initiated in October 1973. There also seems to have been a strong Egyptian belief that Israel could be fought below the nuclear threshold if Arab war aims were limited to the recovery of territory lost in the 1967 war. Some Israeli scholars have specu- lated on the importance of this Arab belief in initiating war against Israel.[9] Additionally, prior to the outbreak of war, at least some senior Egyptian army officers were informed of their government's belief that Israel possessed nuclear weapons. These same officers were informed that the Israelis would only use these systems if the existence of the state was threatened. [10] Such a goal was not part of the Egyptian war plan in 1973.

The fourth major Arab-Israeli war began in October 1973 with Egyptian and Syrian forces launching simultaneous of - fensives into the Sinai desert and Golan Heights, respectively. The Egyptian leadership, as noted, assumed that the fighting could be contained at the conventional level because of limited Arab goals and the strong relationship belligerent Arab states

maintained with the Soviet Union. Some observers also sug -
gested that Cairo maintained its own deterrent. In particular,
it has been suggested that Scud missiles—supplied very reluc
tantly to Egypt by the USSR—helped to give Egypt a theater-
level threat. This threat would not appear serious unless Egypt
used such missiles in conjunction with nonconventional war -
heads, such as nerve or biological agent warheads. Nevertheless,
Scud missiles were then viewed in the West as a system to be
used almost exclusively with nuclear and chemical weapons.

The possible transfer of Soviet nuclear weapons   to Egypt
seems impossible in retrospect but was considered to be   a
serious concern at the time. Two successive November 1973
issues of the usually well-informed journal *Aviation Week &
Space Technology* maintained, for example, that Soviet nuclear
weapons were in Egypt during the war. [11] Later, various indi -
viduals associated with the US government maintained that a
Soviet ship in Alexandria harbor was suspected of carrying
nuclear weapons to Egypt. These suspicions were not con   -
firmed but must have been quite alarming for US and Israeli
decision makers in 1973. [12]

After the Soviet collapse, new evidence has come to light
indicating that the Soviets maintained tight control over even
the conventionally armed Scuds, and that the Egyptians could
not fire these systems without Soviet permission. Such per -
mission was given for two Scud firings only toward the end of
the war when Defense Minister Gennady Grechko ignored the
wishes of Soviet foreign minister Andrei Gromyko on this is -
sue. [13] Such a cautious attitude suggests that the Soviets would
probably not have located nuclear missiles in Egypt even if
they remained under Soviet control.

Contrary to Arab and probably Soviet expectations, the Is -
raelis may have been willing to consider nuclear weapons utili-
zation despite Arab precautions including limited goals, possible deterrent systems, and strong political and military links
with the Soviet Union. The initial Arab successes in the 1973
war are widely reported to have shocked and disoriented the
Israeli leadership to the point that their most basic political
and military assumptions were shattered and no clear alternative paradigm was available to them. According to a 1983 *Time*
magazine report, Defense Minister Moshe Dayan, spoke to Prime

Minister Golda Meir about the possibility of either using nu - clear weapons against the Arabs or facing the prospect of military defeat.[14] The implication is that any option would be preferable to defeat, but Prime Minister Meir did not accept Dayan's reported analysis of the situation. Rather, she chose to rely on the military judgment of two other key military leaders, Lt Gen Chaim Bar-Lev and Lt Gen David Elazar . These generals maintained that the military situation was re - deemable by conventional means.[15]

The uncertainties of Israeli wartime decision-making have been important to the Arab perception of Israel's willingness to use nuclear weapons against them. For example, Mahmoud Karem, the current head of the Egyptian Foreign Ministry's disarmament section, noted in a 1988 book that "it became evident during and following the 1973 Arab-Israeli war that the region came close to the brink of a nuclear exchange." [16] Exchange is an odd choice of word for this situation, and Karem may be maintaining that the Soviet Union would have responded to an Israeli nuclear attack by providing the Arabs with nuclear weapons or attacking Israel itself with nuclear weapons. Both of these scenarios seem unlikely given Soviet alliance behavior. Nevertheless, Karem is expressing a real sense of concern about Egypt's perceived 1973 brush with a nuclear strike.

Also relevant to Egyptian perceptions of the 1973 war are recent comments by Yuval Ne'eman , the former head of the Israeli Atomic Energy Commission (AEC). Ne'eman has stated that Israeli chief of staff Lt Gen David Elazar ordered the deployment of Jericho surface-to-surface missiles without camouflage in 1973 to allow them to be detected by Soviet reconnaissance satellites.[17] Ne'eman noted that it was then "left to the Egyptians" to speculate on what kind of warhead the Jerichos carried and under what conditions they would be used. A long-range system like the Jericho is not a suitable delivery platform for conventional munitions and makes mili - tary sense only with a weapon of mass destruction warhead (be it nuclear, chemical, or biological). The implied threat was therefore unconventional and probably nuclear.

Ne'emen's statement that the Jericho missiles were de ployed to influence the Soviets and through them the Egyptians is probably a distortion. A more likely focus for this presentation was the United States. The United States was undoubtedly encouraged to maintain a strong airlift of conventional weap - ons to Israel by displaying such missiles for US reconnais - sance systems to detect. Yet, Ne'eman is correct in maintain - ing that the deployment of Jericho missiles would have been a matter of deep concern for the Egyptians. It is also an incident that the Egyptian leadership would consider in any postwar assessment of the dangers presented to their country during the fighting.

Following the 1973 war, the Egyptian leadership seemed to realize that Israeli nuclear capabilities (whatever their nature) have to be dealt with in a more realistic manner. One tangible expression of Egyptian concern occurred in 1974 when Egypt and Iran cosponsored a United Nations General Assembly resolution calling for a Middle Eastern nuclear weapons free zone. This resolution passed by the overwhelming margin of 128 to 0 with two abstentions (Israel and Burma) but had no practical effect.[18] More significantly, the postwar diplomatic movements toward Egyptian-Israeli peace increasingly guar - anteed Egyptian security. There is, nevertheless, no evidence that fear of nuclear attack was a significant motivation for Egyptian President Sadat's decision to embark on dramatic new efforts to pursue peace. Sadat, at this point, viewed diplo- macy as the best method to solve Arab-Israeli differences.

Cairo's increased international standing after the Egyptian military's credible performance during the October 1973 war allowed President Sadat more latitude in international affairs. He used this latitude to realign Egypt with the United States and to implement a number of agreements and policies de - signed to move toward a resolution of the Arab-Israeli conflict. These steps included the Sinai I disengagement agreement of 1973, the Sinai II agreement of 1975 , the 1977 Egyptian presidential visit to Jerusalem, the 1978 Camp David Accords, and the 1979 Egyptian-Israeli Peace Treaty. Throughout these negotiations, the issue of nuclear weapons was not publicly raised, although later Egyptian statements claim Sadat ex - pected it to be addressed eventually. If so, he made no visible effort to pressure the Israelis on this issue and was willing to sign an Egyptian-Israeli peace treaty without this issue being addressed or even showing minimal progress. Additionally, Egypt ratified the NPT in February 1981, nine months before Sadat's assassination, in what was probably an effort to bol - ster friendly relationship with the United States. If Sadat was concerned over Israeli nuclear weapons, this was an odd step to take unilaterally.

Interestingly, Israeli journalist Samuel Segev has suggested that some division existed within the Egyptian leadership over the NPT at the time of the Camp David Accords . According to Segev, then Egyptian vice president Mubarak argued against a peace treaty unless the Israelis agreed to join the NPT as a nonnuclear weapons state. Also, according to Segev, Mubarak was strongly supported in this belief by Osama al-Baz, one of Sadat's most trusted foreign policy advisors, who remains im - portant under Mubarak. Sadat overruled objections to the peace process based on NPT-related issues.[19]

The NPT question was clearly subordinated to other regional issues in the years immediately following the March 1979 Egyptian-Israeli Peace Treaty. The nuclear question burst onto the scene again in 1986 following revelations by Israeli nu - clear technician Mordecai Vannunu who suggested that Israel possessed a much larger arsenal of nuclear weapons than previously suspected. The Egyptian Defense Ministry, not sur- prisingly, displayed considerable embarrassment as a result of these disclosures, which suggested that it had been unaware of a key national security threat involving Israel.[20]

Western policies toward Iraqi efforts to produce indigenous nuclear weapons also influenced Egyptian and other Arab at- titudes toward the question of Israel's NPT stance. The Arabs contrasted strong Western concerns about Iraq beginning in the 1980s with the relaxed attitude taken toward Israeli nu - clear activities. Many Arabs viewed the mild Western response to the 1981 Israeli destruction of the Tuwaitha reactor in Iraq as unsatisfactory for that reason, and the charge of a double standard was continually raised. These complaints became muted shortly after the Iraqi invasion of Kuwait and the 1991 Gulf War, but concerns about Israeli nuclear capabilities and the lack of a meaningful Arab counterweight to Israeli nuclear capabilities were never fully dismissed. More recently, signifi - cant elements of Arab public opinion have been enraged b y the continuing sanctions and air strikes directed at Iraq for its efforts to retain some of its weapons of mass destruction (WMD) capability. These Arab critics suggest that while Iraq is placed under both economic sanctions and military attack to ensure its nonnuclear non-WMD status, Israel is not even seriously pressured.[21]

Mubarak Challenges Israel over Nuclear Weapons

President Sadat's successor, Hosni Mubarak , for the most part ignored the issue of Israeli nuclear weapons   for the first nine years of his presidency but signaled an abrupt policy change on 8 April 1990, announcing his own plan for a Middle Eastern weapons of mass destruction free zone (WMDFZ). The Mubarak Initiative called for: (1) the removal of all nuclear, chemical, and biological weapons from the Middle East, (2) the inclusion of all regional countries in this initiative, with (3) verification procedures applied to all countries in the region.[22] This initiative was announced five days after a speech by President Saddam Hussein of Iraq in which he threatened to "make Israel eat fire" with binary chemical weapons if it "tries anything against Iraq."[23]

Saddam's reckless words provided Mubarak with an oppor - tunity to present a refined but still vague version of the 1974 UN General Assembly resolution as a response to the problem of Middle Eastern strategic posturing with WMD. Not surpris - ingly, the Mubarak plan won Arab and international praise but did not provoke any changes in Israel's approach to secu - rity issues. The Israeli leadership's only official comments on their own suspected nuclear capability occurred when they occasionally promised terrible and disproportionate punish - ment to any country that attacks Israel with chemical or bio - logical weapons. These hints were often so apocalyptic that a nonnuclear interpretation is difficult if not impossible.[24]

Egyptian foreign minister Amre Moussa   used the an - nouncement of the Mubarak plan as a starting point for   a continuing effort to express Egyptian concerns about Israeli nonmembership in the NPT. By 1991 he began stating that Middle Eastern arms control measures could not have serious value in the absence of some effort to address the issue of Israeli nuclear weapons. Such differences over arms control did not unravel the Egyptian-Israeli working relationship on key bilateral issues.[25] The post-Gulf War Middle East peace process moved forward with strong Egyptian and Israeli participation and support.[26]

In addition to bilateral negotiations between Arab and Israeli parties, the Middle East peace process (begun at Madrid in 1991) created multilateral forums for the discussion of important regional issues including environment, economics, refugees, water and arms control, and regional security (ACRS). The ACRS meetings, which began in early 1992, became an important forum for Egypt to voice its concerns about the Israeli nuclear program.[27] These same concerns were also raised in the supporting conferences designated as ACRS Track 2. The ACRS Track 2 meetings were informal and designed to provide scholarly and expert input into the ACRS Track 1 functions as well as to allow for more open discussion of key issues among the diplomats who were freed from the requirements of formal negotiations.

Throughout the first few years of the ACRS talks, Egyptian spokesmen strongly maintained that Israeli membership in the NPT was a central requirement for regional security. Yet, while this issue was given strong emphasis, the Egyptians had not yet reached the point where they treated it as the only arms control issue worthy of discussion. It was therefore during the first few years of the ACRS meetings that the greatest amount of progress occurred on nonnuclear issues such as maritime security, search and rescue cooperation, and the exchange of military data.[28] While such agreements hardly constitute dramatic arms control such as the downsizing of military forces and the destruction of weapons, they do constitute a beginning, and the prospects of other CSBMs occurring were a reality.

The movement of ACRS toward the negotiation of additional CSBMs was disrupted by a series of international agreements involving global arms control. The opening of the Chemical Weapons Convention (CWC) for signature in January 1993 was the first major agreement to create reverberations for the ACRS talks by altering the context of Egyptian foreign policy.[29]

This problem occurred because the CWC raised important strategic considerations bearing directly on Egyptian-Israeli disagreements over nuclear weapons. Many Arabs considered chemical weapons to be the only plausible near-term military deterrent to an Israeli nuclear strike. To abolish chemical weapons globally while leaving the Israeli nuclear issue unaddressed seemed a formula to institutionalize Israeli strategic dominance. For some states, such as Egypt, this disparity in strategic power was viewed primarily as influencing the issue of diplomatic and political leverage. Other states, and most especially Syria, had leaderships that were concerned about maintaining a chemical weapons-based deterrent for national security reasons.[30]

Egypt correspondingly announced that it would not sign the CWC, and the Egyptian leadership urged other Arab states to follow Cairo's lead on this issue.[31] Concerns about Israeli strategic dominance as well as Egyptian diplomatic pressure limited the number of Arab CWC signatories. Israeli foreign minister Shimon Peres, conversely, did sign the CWC, and at the January 1993 signing ceremony called for negotiations among all regional states to establish peaceful relations with Israel and enter into negotiations on a Middle Eastern WMDFZ.[32] The Egyptians viewed this offer as insufficient or even a delaying tactic because it was conditioned on other regional states becoming parties to the Middle East peace process. Peres's proposal suggested that nuclear disarmament could come only after such nations as Syria, Iran, Iraq, and Libya have become accepted partners in the peace process. The near-term impossibility of this occurring seemed to defer Israeli disarmament issues indefinitely. Much later, in a reflection of the continuing deadlock over arms control, the Israelis made a September 1997 announcement that they would not ratify the CWC because of a lack of progress on regional chemical disarmament.[33]

In the aftermath of the conflict over the CWC, Egypt began to display a greater unwillingness to support the ACRS process because of the issue of Israeli nuclear weapons . Correspondingly, Cairo moved to block any discussion of nonnuclear issues in ACRS and, in doing so, produced a deadlock on further progress on CSBMs. As a result of Egyptian action, no further ACRS plenary sessions were held from December 1994

onward. At the time of this writing, it seems extremely un -
likely that they will resume. The ACRS intercessionals, which
dealt with specific arms control CSBMs, lasted longer, and
meetings continued for some time after the collapse of the
plenary sessions with only limited progress. ACRS Track 2,
while unofficial, became more important as it was the only
forum not deadlocked.[34]

While part of the motivation for Egypt's hard-line policies
may have been residual bitterness over CWC issues, a more
important reason was undoubtedly the approach of the NPT
review conference. This conference, which according to the
treaty text was to occur 25 years after the treaty entered into
force, was to decide the future of the NPT. Accordingly, the
treaty could be allowed to expire; it could be extended for a
fixed time period of either long or short duration, or it could be
extended indefinitely. Only treaty parties were allowed to send
delegates to the conference, which ensured Israeli nonpartici -
pation. Nevertheless, the Israelis were deeply interested in the
outcome of these proceedings. They hoped to see the NPT ex tended
for other states, while they remained free of its restrictions.

Harsh and frequent Egyptian criticism of Israeli nonmem -
bership in the NPT failed to gain any concessions from Israel
as the date of the NPT Review Conference approached. In early
1995, then Foreign Minister Peres set the tone for future Is -
raeli responses by noting that "we are not looking for a fight
with Egypt, but this [NPT membership with an attendant re -
quirement for nuclear disarmament] is a very serious issue,
and Israel will maintain its deterrent ambiguity."[35] Peres also
maintained that Israel could not discuss major disarmament
issues before a comprehensive peace accord had been estab -
lished in the region. He further maintained that there was "no
room for Israeli gestures on the nuclear issue."[36] This position
was a rejection of the Egyptian arguments at their most basic
level. Also such statements, articulated by a leading Israeli
dove, made it clear that Israel would not compromise on this
issue. Cairo correspondingly prepared for diplomatic battle in
New York.

As the NPT Extension Conference approached, Egyptian
Foreign Ministry officials made a number of statements sup -
porting the goals of regional and global nonproliferation. Cairo

expressed agreement with the principle of global nonproliferation but also maintained that the NPT could not be extended
indefinitely with all of its "loopholes" and "shortcomings" in -
tact. NPT supporters viewed these statements with some con -
cern and were particularly worried that Cairo might lead a
Third World voting bloc opposed to the indefinite extension of
the NPT. As the conference became imminent, the Egyptians
clearly hoped that proarms control states, including the
United States, would exert pressure on Israel to make NPT-related concessions. Israel, more correctly, never expected seri -
ous pressure from the United States on nuclear issues.

Additionally, the Egyptians believed that Israel   itself had
benefited from the NPT , which led to the application of an
antiproliferation norm throughout the region. Cairo may, there -
fore, have hoped that Israel would make concessions to ensure
that the treaty was extended indefinitely. The concession that
was of the greatest interest to Egypt was an Israeli commit   -
ment to join the NPT at a future date. Using somewhat surreal
logic, the Egyptians also maintained that Israeli acceptance of
the NPT and full International Atomic Energy Agency (IAEA)
safeguards would create the conditions for the entry of other
Arab states into arms control discussions. Israel, of course,
recognized the unlikelihood that such actions would even
slightly influence Syria, let alone more radical states such as
Libya, Iran, and Iraq. These countries clearly had other major
differences with Israel that had nothing to do with the NPT.[37]

The New York conference ended in a major victory for the
supporters of indefinite NPT extension despite intensive Egyp -
tian lobbying. A number of states including Canada and
South Africa played major roles in supporting indefinite NPT
extension. The Canadians were particularly effective at coordi-
nating support for the treaty, while the South Africans used
their moral authority as a state which had destroyed its own
nuclear weapons to call for indefinite extension of the NPT. In
the final act of the conference, the NPT was extended indefi   -
nitely by acclamation.[38]

After the New York conference, the Egyptian government
and media attempted to put the best face possible on their
diplomatic defeat. The Egyptians maintained that they had
never expected to win the struggle against the combined diplo-

matic clout of the United States and its allies, but they hoped to make their case as strongly as possible. The Egyptian diplomatic defeat in New York was nevertheless real and undoubtedly somewhat humiliating. It did not, however, lead Cairo to give up on the NPT issue as most Israelis hoped.

After Egypt's New York Defeat
New Problems for the Peace Process

In November 1995 a Jewish religious zealot opposed to the peace process assassinated Israeli prime minister Yitzhak Rabin. The murder shocked Cairo, and the Egyptian leadership understood that the political situation now called for political restraint. On 6 November Mubarak made his first trip to Israel since assuming the presidency to attend Rabin's funeral where he gave a brief but laudatory eulogy for the prime minister.[39] The new acting Israeli prime minister Shimon Peres immediately reiterated his interest in peace and even made some cryptic remarks on nuclear weapons stating in December, "Give me peace, and we will give up the atom."[40] This was an interesting statement, although it did not really go beyond his CWC speech in 1993.

In response to the new situation, Mubarak and Moussa relaxed their criticisms of a variety of Israeli policies including those related to the NPT . In the first few months of 1996, Moussa only occasionally commented on Israeli nuclear weapons issues. In April 1996, less than one month prior to the Israeli elections, the international situation changed, and the Egyptians felt the need to once again raise the issue of Israeli nuclear weapons. The occasion for this return to the hard line was the signing ceremony for the Treaty of Pelindaba, which established a nuclear-weapons-free zone for Africa. The ceremonies for this treaty were held in Cairo where Egypt hosted delegates from 43 nations.[41] The choice of Cairo as the setting for the ceremony also helped to underscore Cairo's special leadership role (since the time of President Nasser) on questions of global disarmament.

Once again Mubarak and Moussa felt that Egypt needed to show leadership in criticizing Israel's refusal to join the NPT. For Cairo to fail to do so would have appeared to many ob   -

servers as a compromise of Egypt's most basic foreign policy principles. Moussa, therefore, forcefully raised the issue.[42] Unfortunately, three days after the signing ceremony, Egyptian-Israeli relations were subjected to an additional shock as the result of the Israeli military incursion into Lebanon known as "Operation Grapes of Wrath." This assault began on 14 April 1996 and continued for 17 days. Egypt's inability to curb the actions of an Israeli government led by Peres may have caused Cairo embarrassment with other Arab states and also its own population.[43]

As difficult as the Lebanon incursion was for Egyptian-Israeli relations, a more severe jolt occurred in May 1996 when the Likud Party leader Benyamin Netanyahu was elected Israeli prime minister. Arab reaction to this event ranged from concern to shock due to Netanyahu's harsh rhetoric against the Palestinians and the peace process. To address these issues, Egyptian strategy called for even more assertive diplomacy to pressure Netanyahu on peace-related issues and essentially make him over into someone more like Peres. This logic was flawed not only because of Netanyahu's commitment to highly nationalistic principles but also because his power base lay firmly within the conservative wing of the Israeli political system including West Bank settlers. Netanyahu could not make significant concessions for peace without losing support in the Cabinet, Knesset, and among the conservatives of the general public.

Prime Minister Netanyahu 's vision for peace was correspondingly irreconcilable with Egyptian and other Arab expectations for the requirements of the peace process. The Egyptian response to the inevitable disagreements with the new government as it began its tenure was typically harsh. In the aftermath of Netanyahu's election, Foreign Minister Moussa remained a leading critic of Israel with his central theme being that the new government was not implementing agreements that had already been concluded, and that this tendency would destroy the peace process if it was left uncorrected. Mubarak also doubted Netanyahu 's good faith and stated, "I hope that at least once in my life I will be able to believe him."[44] Jordan, by contrast, made a strong initial effort to work with the new government, but this strategy proved ineffective as well. King ibn Talal Hussein later publicly charged that Netanyahu was not interested in peace.[45]

In the period following the Netanyahu election, Egyptian-Is - raeli relations declined for reasons largely unrelated to the NPT. In particular, strong differences developed over Jerusa - lem building projects, West Bank settlements, continuing Is - raeli military activities in Lebanon, and a series of new bilat - eral issues (such as the capture and later conviction of an alleged Israeli spy in Egypt). The never-gentle Egyptian press sharpened its anti-Israeli tone in response to these problems and by doing so further angered the Israelis.[46]

The possibility of an improvement in Egyptian -Israeli rela - tions was also partially undermined by the view of hard-line Egyptians and other Arabs that any strengthening of relations was a concession to Israel by the Arab states. The Egyptians stated that Israel had already received numerous economic and other normalization advantages without giving much in return, and this could not continue. Harsher critics such as Syrian defense minister, Gen Mustafa Tlas, went even further stating that "Arabs must stop making gratuitous concessions to Israeli leaders such as normalization measures and coop - eration projects."[47] Unfortunately, this type of logic means that the extremes of both sides will feed off of each other's negative actions while cooperative actions that build trust and break down stereotypes will not occur.

Israeli Reaction to Egyptian Antinuclear Diplomacy

The Israeli response to Egypt's assertive diplomacy on the NPT was predictable given the deep Israeli sensitivity about national security issues, and Israeli military doctrine stressing that wars must be won rapidly, with limited casualties, and on enemy soil. Indeed, Israelis seem comfortable only when they maintain overwhelming military superiority over the combined strength of all potential regional adversaries. Likewise, an ex - ceptionally broad spectrum of the Israeli leadership and pub lic remains concerned over the danger of Arab conventional at - tacks and usually views worst case analysis of enemy capa bili- ties as prudent. This highly conservative method of analysis has come into direct conflict with the Egyptian approach, which remains skeptical of Israel's conceptions of its national security requirements.

The 1991 Gulf War also reinforced some traditional Israeli beliefs about the value of nuclear weapons in a Middle East - ern regional context. In particular, Iraqi conventional missile attacks on Israeli cities supported the Israeli belief about the importance of even an implied nuclear deterrent capability. Rightly or wrongly, the Israeli public generally assumed that Saddam refrained from using chemically armed Scuds against Israeli cities in the Gulf War due to the Israeli nuclear deter - rent rather than any technical or command and control short- comings associated with the use of chemical warheads.[48] Rich- ard Cheney, then US secretary of defense, had even stated publicly that he expected an Israeli WMD response to any use of chemical weapons against Israeli targets, which reinforced the idea that Saddam was deterred by the threat of nuclear weapons.[49] Egyptian demands that Israel renounce its nuclear option are correspondingly viewed in Israel as so unreason - able that they have been rejected across the Israeli political spectrum. This solidarity strongly contrasts with clear Israeli divisions on other peace-related issues such as the expansion of settlements on the West Bank or the security implications of a Palestinian state.

In contrast to the Israelis, virtually no Egyptian or other Arab leader believes that Israel has an indefinite right to maintain overwhelming military superiority in the region. In - stead, Egypt calls for "strategic balance " rather than security that is guaranteed "for only one country."[50] Additionally, most Arabs do not view Israeli strategic superiority as a strictly defensive asset. Rather, they are concerned that in the wrong hands such superiority has and will continue to lead to the casual, disproportionate, and reflexive Israeli use of conven - tional forces against neighbors such as Syria and Lebanon.

Arab-Israeli disagreements over strategic issues are there- fore virtually guaranteed by radical differences in outlooks over regional security. Aggravating the situation further for Cairo has been a continuing series of Israeli diplomatic pro - tests about Egyptian military procurement. The Egyptians view these complaints as indicating an excessive and unrea -

sonable desire to keep Egypt militarily weak. The Israelis have also protested loudly about Egyptian acquisition of conven - tional missiles and other weapons systems.[51] Such complaints underscore Israel's insistence on strategic superiority and are highly irritating to the Egyptians. Cairo, as a strong aspirant for Arab leadership, feels that a powerful military is essential to support that claim. Foreign Minister Moussa has called Is- raeli statements about Egyptian weapons procurement "inex - cusable" in light of the Israeli possession of nuclear weapons.[52]

Differing Egyptian and Israeli attitudes toward regional se - curity can also be seen in the two countries' contrasting reac - tions to the nuclear weapons activities of radical Middle Eastern states. The first important example of this divergence involved Iraqi nuclear weapons activity. Senior Egyptian foreign minis - try official Nabil Fahmy maintained that Israel was mistaken to question the IAEA's ability to monitor weapons activities in Iraq since the IAEA was the international instrument estab - lished to do so by the world community. Instead, Fahmy main- tained that Israel was the problem for Middle Eastern security since it would not join the NPT and would not place its own facilities under IAEA safeguards. The assessment regarding Iraq was, of course, proven incorrect in the aftermath of the 1990–91 Gulf War when a massive Iraqi nuclear weapons program was discovered successfully hidden from the IAEA. The Israelis must have considered Fahmy's approach naïve and legalistic at best, and reckless and hostile at worst. [53] It is also interesting that in the aftermath of the Gulf War, Fahmy's previous statements did not embarrass him and did not harm his career. Instead, he became the head of the Egyptian ACRS delegation and remained deeply involved with arms control issues until his 1997 appointment as ambassador to Japan.

In the aftermath of the 1991 Gulf War, Egypt also remained skeptical about Israel's public concerns that Iran might ac - quire a nuclear weapons option. Egyptian diplomatic praise for Iran being a member of the NPT and the previous instance of Baghdad circumventing this treaty seem to have had no influence on Egyptian logic. At various times, Moussa went even further in his rhetoric than simply dismissing the Iranian threat. Sometimes he seems willing to justify the activities of other regional states seeking to acquire WMD systems stating, for example, "We cannot blame anyone in the region for ac - quiring nuclear know-how to protect himself as long as Is - rael's nuclear program exists."[54] While Egypt's leadership does not favor Iranian acquisition of nuclear weapons, they never - theless seem reluctant to treat this possibility with the same concern as the Israeli nuclear weapons option, and the Egyp - tians appear especially wary about allowing the Iranian threat to become a justification for Israeli nuclear weapons. It should also be noted that Egyptian policy on this point is inconsistent since President Mubarak has repeatedly expressed his deep concerns about the "danger" posed by any future Iranian ac - quisition of nuclear weapons. Mubarak has been described by subordinates as having a "deep personal distrust of Iran.[55]

Egyptian Domestic Politics and the Israeli Nuclear Issue

Egyptian domestic politics have influenced the NPT debate as well as Israeli politics. In particular, domestic factors have made it difficult for President Mubarak to retreat from NPT-re- lated demands once they were made. In general, this situation has occurred because the Egyptian public respects Mubarak as a skilled foreign policy president who is important on the world stage. Thus, Mubarak's foreign policy is an important resource, and he loathes appearing weak or easily intimidated in his interactions with the Israelis.

President Mubarak's reputation as an authoritative and as- tute foreign policy leader is also vital to him because his government has not always been successful if judged on such key domestic issues as the performance of Egypt's economy and progress toward democratization. Additionally, Mubarak has refused to designate a vice president and successor al - though the president is entering his early seventies. These problems may create a need for foreign policy victories to compensate for other shortcomings.

A key priority in Mubarak's foreign policy thinking has been Cairo's traditional role as a leader of the Arab World and the developing nations in general. President Nasser was especially successful at asserting Egyptian regional leadership and also became one of the central figures in the nonaligned movement in the 1950s and the 1960s. Although nonalignment is often viewed as a dated concept in the post-cold-war world, it is still popular in Egypt, and the Egyptian press often emphasizes that Cairo still acts on behalf of the nonaligned movement. Mubarak's ability to appear as a regional rather than simply an Egyptian leader is a factor that boosts his standing with the Egyptian public.

The Mubarak government is also aware that most ordinary Egyptians view the Israeli possession of nuclear weapons with disapproval, and that Israel itself is deeply unpopular within some elements of Egyptian society. [56] This hostility sharpened with the May 1996 election of Prime Minister Netanyahu. After Netanyahu's decision to build the Har Homa settlement in East Jerusalem, Mubarak had to fend off strong domestic criticism for refusing to freeze relations with Israel. Mubarak's supporters, while also critical of Israel, maintained that such reactions would simply alienate the United States.

Many Israelis have personalized the problems with Egypt by blaming Foreign Minister Moussa for bad relations (although he was clearly acting on behalf of President Mubarak). Some Israelis have also begun referring to Moussa as a "Nasserist" or a "neo-Nasserist," and by doing so identified him with the memory of one of Israel's most uncompromising historical op - ponents. The Israelis' charges were made on the basis of Moussa's orientation toward the Third World, caution about Western motives in the Middle East, interest in Arab leader - ship, and strong criticism of Israel. Also, Moussa established his own links to the Nasser family when his daughter, Hania, married Nasser's grandson, Ahmad Asharaf Marawan, in an elaborate ceremony on the Nile in May 1997.[57]

Moussa, nevertheless, has some key policy orientations that are clearly distinguishable from Nasserism. In particular he does not share Nasser's penchant to call for military solutions to Arab-Israeli differences, and he does not favor a return to the debilitating policies of "Arab cold war" where hostile invec - tive against other Arab states (often over insufficient commit - ment to the cause of Palestine) was a standard part of the political landscape. Additionally, Moussa's desire for Egypt to play a leadership role in the Arab World is hardly a principle exclusive to "Nasserism." Furthermore, Moussa was highly cooperative with the Israeli leadership in the early 1990s when Egypt had a more prominent role in the peace process.[58] These distinctions are insufficient for his Israeli critics who point to his contemporary role as one of Israel's toughest critics.

Foreign Minister Moussa's criticism of the Israeli nuclear program has almost always led to a favorable portrayal in the Egyptian press. The flamboyant, fierce style of his speeches against the NPT may have been designed to attract the favorable attention of the press, which they often did. It has also led to a situation where Moussa has become the most popular member of the cabinet and the individual least vulnerable to replacement in Mubarak's periodic cabinet reshuffles.

Netanyahu, in response to poor Egyptian-Israeli relations, repeatedly called upon the Egyptian government to curb their press and embark upon a program to "educate the public for peace." Mubarak skillfully deflected these concerns by pointing to hostile Israeli press stories about him. He also stated that the *Jerusalem Post* "frequently offends me with its awful and terrible cartoons" and its "very, very impolite articles."[59] In an argument not made by President Mubarak, it might also be noted that the Egyptian press has numerous eccentric, conspiracy-oriented stories involving a number of countries, although Israel is often singled out for special enmity.

Conclusion—The Continuing Conflict

The Egyptian-Israeli interaction over nuclear weapons issues indicates a complete lack of understanding between the parties. During the Rabin-Peres era, there was an Israeli effort to find a compromise based on cosmetic concessions to Egyptian sensitivities. This strategy was ineffective because Cairo would not accept minor concessions that would essentially allow the Israelis to maintain the status quo. Currently, both leaderships seem to be speaking predominantly to their own publics and the international press in an effort to blame the other side for the breakdown in arms control negotiations. There is also something of a vicious circle that has developed with Egypt criticizing Israel, Israel attempting to contain Egyptian influence, and Egypt then complaining about the process of marginalization.

The timing of the ACRS talks, CWC negotiations, NPT Extension Conference, and the conclusion of the Pelindaba Treaty breathed life into the Egyptian antinuclear crusade. It was perhaps especially unfortunate that the 25th anniversary of the NPT (with the requisite extension conference) intersected with an especially delicate stage of the Middle East peace pro-cess. Nevertheless, the passing of the NPT Extension Conference into history has not led to a softening of the Egyptian line on this issue. Indeed, Egypt has continued to criticize Israel's refusal to join the NPT in stark and decisive terms in the post-1995 time frame.

It is also interesting that the Egyptian-Israeli language of diplomatic discourse over the nuclear issue remains quite different. Egypt often makes political and legal arguments centering on the need for universal adherence to treaties, the need for regional equality, and the requirement for respecting the rights of sovereign nations. Israel, on the other hand, justifies its nonmembership on political and military grounds.

Neither side is prepared to concede that its rival has correctly framed the question or is giving due consideration to the most important variables. It therefore seems likely that Egyptian-Israeli differences over NPT-related issues will continue, and arms control talks in the Middle East will be constrained by these problems.

The continuing instances of both sides talking past each other also suggest that there is a strong need for discussions of these issues among Egyptian and Israeli arms control professionals. While actual agreements over nuclear arms control may be a distant goal, it is useful for both sides to continue their interaction and discussions of arms control perceptions and priorities. For this reason the ACRS Track II negotiations seem to be an especially important forum to be maintained and supported. Arms control by its nature is almost always difficult, and cannot be abandoned in the face of serious problems. Continuing dialogue can help provide a foundation by which Egypt and Israel start to move beyond the emotionally charged rhetoric that has been so prominent in this debate.

Notes

1. Gregory L. Aftandilian, *Egypt's Bid for Arab Leadership: Implications for US Policy* (New York: Council on Foreign Relations Press, 1993), 27, 33–34.

2. Robert Springborg, "Egypt: Repressions Toll," *Current History,* January 1998, 32–37.

3. Fawaz A. Gerges, "Egyptian-Israeli Relations Turn Sour," *Foreign Affairs,* May–June 1995, 69–78.

4. Shai Feldman and Abdullah Toukan, *Bridging the Gap: A Future Security Architecture for the Middle East* (New York: Rowman & Littlefield 1997), 80–82.

5. Avner Cohen, *Israel and the Bomb* (New York: Columbia University Press, 1998), 243–46.

6. Yair Evron, *Israel's Nuclear Dilemma* (Ithaca, N. Y.: Cornell University Press, 1994), 14–20.

7. Cohen, 259.

8. Cohen, 259; Avner Cohen, "Cairo, Dimona and the June 1967 War," *Middle East*; and Pierre Pean, *Les Deux Bombs* (Libraire Artheme Fayard, 1982) (in French).

9. Martin van Creveld, *Nuclear Proliferation and the Future of Conflict* (New York: Free Press, 1993), 109.

10. Author's interview with retired Egyptian Major General. Conducted in Amman, Jordan September 1998.

11. Cecil Brownlow, "Soviets Poise Three Front Global Drive," *Aviation Week & Space Technology,* 5 November 1973, 12–14; and "Washington Roundup," *Aviation Week & Space Technology,* 12 November 1973, 11.

12. William B. Quandt, "Soviet Policy in the October Middle East War–II," *International Affairs,* October 1977, 596–97; and Yona Bandmann and Yishai Cordova, "The Soviet Nuclear Threat Towards the Close of the Yom Kippur War," *The Jerusalem Journal of International Relations* 5, no. 1 (1980): 94–110.

13. Viktor Israelian, *Inside the Kremlin During the Yom Kippur War* (University Park, Pa.: Pennsylvania University Press, 1995), 143.

14. "How Israel Got the Bomb," *Time,* 12 April 1976, 39.

15. Donald Neff, *Warriors Against Israel* (Brattleboro, Vt.: Amana Books, 1988), 156–58; and Robert Slater, *Warrior Statesman: The Life of Moshe Dayan* (New York: St. Martin's Press, 1991), 354–66.

16. Mahmoud Karem, *A Nuclear Weapons Free Zone in the Middle East: Problems and Prospects* (New York: Greenwood Press, 1988), 93.

17. "Yuval Ne'eman: 'During the Yom Kippur War we deployed Jericho missiles and left it to the Egyptians to guess what they were carrying,'" *Ha'aretz,* 23 May 1997.

18. Karem, 96.

19. Samuel Segev, *Crossing the Jordan: Israel's Hard Road to Peace* (New York: St. Martin's Press, 1998), 269.

20. Evron, 18–20; Martin van Creveld, *The Sword and the Olive: A Critical History of the Israeli Defense Forces* (New York: Public Affairs, 1998), 280–81; and Daniel Raviv and Yossi Melman, *Every Spy a Prince: The Complete History of Israel's Intelligence Community* (Boston: Houghton Mifflin, 1990), 360–78.

21. "Mubarak Urges Clinton to Halt Airstrikes," *Arab News,* 20 December 1998, 3; and "Moussa Says Butler Should Be Replaced," *Arab News,* 22 December 1998, 3.

22. Shai Feldman, *Nuclear Weapons and Arms Control in the Middle East* (Cambridge: MIT Press, 1997), 226–28; and Mohamed Nabil Fahmy, "Egypt's Disarmament Initiative," *The Bulletin of the Atomic Scientists,* November 1990, 10.

23. "Iraqi Domestic Service," Foreign Broadcast Information Service (FBIS), *Daily Report on the Middle East and South Asia,* 3 April 1990, 32–35.

24. Feldman, 102.

25. John R. Redick, "Regional Nuclear Restraint: Towards a Nuclear-Free Zone in the Middle East," *Middle East Insight,* January–February 1995, 59. See Abdulhay Sayed, "The Future of Israeli Nuclear Force and the Middle East Peace Process,"*Security Dialogue,* March 1997, 31–48.

26. Uri Savir, *The Process:1,100 Days that Changed the Middle East* (New York: Random House, 1998).

27. Dalia Dassa Kaye, "Madrid's Forgotten Forum, The Middle East Multilaterals," *Washington Quarterly,* Winter 1997, 167–86.

28. Feldman and Toukan, 80–82.

29. Dany Shoham, "Chemical and Biological Weapons in Egypt," *The Nonproliferation Review,* Spring–Summer 1998, 52–53.

30. M. Zuhair Diab, "Syria's Chemical and Biological Weapons: Assessing Capabilities and Motivations," *The Nonproliferation Review,* Fall 1997, 104–11; and Zvi Bar'el, "Who has the Stronger Weapon," *Ha'aretz,* 4 May 1997.

31. Shoham, 52–53.

32. Gerald M. Steinberg, "Deterrence and Middle East Stability: An Israeli Perspective," *Security Dialogue,* March 1997, 51–52.

33. "Israel Refuses to Ratify Weapons Ban Treaty," *Arab News,* 5 September 1997, 5.

34. Peter Jones, "Arms Control in the Middle East: Some Reflections on ACRS," *Security Dialogue,* March 1997, 57–70; and Ehud Yaari, "Track II," *Jerusalem Report,* 26 June 1997, 24.

35. "Israel Will Not Sign NPT, Asserts Peres," *Arab News,* 2 February 1995, 9.

36. "Egypt Awaits Israeli Gesture on NPT," *Arab News,* 14 March 1995, 9.

37. "To Sign Or Not To Sign: Israel Embattled Over NPT Refusal," *Jane's Defence Weekly,* 25 March 1995, 22.

38. Helen Leigh-Phippard, "Multilateral Diplomacy at the 1995 NPT Review and Extension Conference," *Diplomacy and Statescraft* 8, no. 2 (July 1997): 167–90.

39. "Eulogy for the Late Prime Minister and Defense Minister Yitzhak Rabin by Egyptian President Hosni Mubarak," Mt. Herzl, Jerusalem, 6 November 1995, Israeli Ministry of Foreign Affairs Home Page on the Internet.

40. Steve Rodan, "Clear and Present Option," *Jerusalem Post International Edition,* 29 June 1996, 18.

41. Bereng Mtimkulu, "Africa Bans the Bomb," *The Bulletin of the Atomic Scientists,* July–August 1996, 11; and Savita Pande, "Treaty of Pelindaba: How Different?" *Strategic Analysis,* July 1998, 547–59.

42. Cairo MENA, "Musa, IAEA's Blix Comment on African Treaty," FBIS, *Daily Report: Near East, South Asia,* 11 April 1996.

43. Andrew Album, "Against All Odds: Peres Bows Out," *The Middle East,* July–August 1996, 5.

44. "Mubarak Accuses Netanyahu of Lying," *Arab News,* 2 April 1997, 3.

45. "Bibi Under Attack," *The Economist,* 15 March 1997, 42; and "Jordanian King Says He Mistrusts Netanyahu," *Arab News,* 2 November 1997, 4.

46. Khalid Amayreh, "Israel Angry with 'Anti-Semitism' in Egyptian Paper," *Arab News,* 10 March 1997, 4; and "Israel Complains to Egypt over Trial," *Arab News,* 21 May 1997, 3.

47. "Mubarak: Israeli Attitude Will Lead to Disaster," *Arab News,* 7 October 1996, 3.

48. Moshe Arens, *Broken Covenant, American Foreign Policy and the Crisis Between the US and Israel*(New York: Simon & Schuster, 1995), 216.

49. Shai Feldman, "Israeli Deterrence and the Gulf War," in *War in the Gulf: Implications for Israel,* ed. Joseph Alpher (Boulder, Colo.: Westview Press, 1992), 202.

50. Lima Nabil, "Musa Discusses Peace Process," *Amman Al-Ray,* 12 February 1997, FBIS Internet site.

51. Cairo Arab Republic of Egypt Radio Network, "Musa Comments on Korean Missiles, Summit, Israeli Stance," FBIS, *Daily Report, Near East, South Asia,* 30 June 1997, Internet edition; and John Lancaster, "Mubarak to Netanyahu: Help Me, I'll Help You," *Washington Post,* 23 July 1996, A–12.

52. Cairo MENA, interview with Foreign Minister Musa [Moussa]," *Daily Report: Near East, South Asia,* 7 July 1996, Internet edition.

53. Mohammed Nabil Fahmy, "Controlling Weapons of Mass Destruction in the Middle East," *Arab-American Affairs,* Winter 1990–1991, 126–34.

54. Farid Wajds, Amr Musa: "Region's Future Depends on Balance and Understanding between Its Countries," *Al Ahram,* 24 January 1996, 9. (Arabic).

55. Feldman, 133.

56. Aftandilian, 62–64.

57. "Nasser's Grandson Weds Daughter of Egyptian Foreign Minister," *Arab News,* 25 May 1997, 15.

58. Ranan Laurie, "Egypt's President Opens His Heart," *The Jerusalem Report,* 3 April 1997, 22–26.

59. Margot Dudkevitch, "Egypt Would Welcome Sharon as Foreign Minister," *Jerusalem Post International Edition,* 17 October 1998, 32.

Contributors

Dr. Avner Cohen is a senior fellow at the National Security Archives in Washington, D.C. Formerly, Dr. Cohen was a senior fellow at the US Institute of Peace and co-director of the Project on Nuclear Arms Control in the Middle East at the Defense and Arms Control Studies (DACS) program at Massachusetts Institute of Technology (1990–95). Before his arrival in Washington, Cohen completed his study on the political history of the Israeli nuclear program, *Israel and the Bomb*, published by Columbia University Press in 1998. For more than a decade, Dr. Cohen has written on issues related to nuclear weapons, primarily on the questions of nuclear deterrence and morality as well as issues related to nuclear proliferation in the Middle East.

Anthony H. Cordesman is currently a senior fellow at the Center for Strategic and International Studies and co-director of the Middle East Program. He is also a military analyst for the American Broadcasting Company (ABC) where he acted as national security analyst for ABC News during the Gulf War. He has served in senior positions in the Office of the Secretary of Defense, the State Department, the Department of Energy, and the Defense Advanced Research Projects Agency. Cordesman has written and lectured extensively on the Middle East and the Gulf and other national security issues. He is the author of 15 books on Middle East military issues and has written several others on foreign policy problems outside that region. In addition, he has written numerous magazine and newspaper articles, and has often appeared on radio and television. He was formerly the international editor of the *Armed Forces Journal* and US editor of *Armed Forces* (UK).

Dr. Ibrahim A. Karawan is the associate director of the Middle East Center at the University of Utah and a member of the faculty. Between 1995 and 1997 he was the senior fellow for Middle East Security and a directing staff member at the International Institute for Strategic Studies (IISS) in London. He is also a former senior research associate at the Al-Ahram Center for Political and Strategic Studies in Cairo, Egypt. His published work focused on the political role of Arab military establishments, inter-Arab relations, nuclear weapons and Middle

Eastern conflicts, Egyptian foreign and defense policies, and the politics of Islamic resurgence in the Arab world. His most recent publication is *The Islamist Impasse* (New York: Oxford University Press, 1997).

Dr. Lawrence Scheinman is currently distinguished professor of International Policy and director of the Washington, D.C., office of the Monterey Institute of International Studies. He is the former assistant director (assistant secretary) for Non-Proliferation and Regional Arms Control of the United States Arms Control and Disarmament Agency (ACDA), a post to which he was appointed by President Clinton in 1994 and held through late 1997. He is also emeritus professor at Cornell University where he taught international law and relations and served as director of the Program on Science, Technology and Society, and as director and later associate director of the Peace Studies Program. Dr. Scheinman was a member of the tenured faculty at the University of Michigan and the University of California, Los Angeles, before joining Cornell University. He is also currently an adjunct professor in the School of Foreign Service at Georgetown University. He holds a PhD and an MA from the University of Michigan, a JD from New York University School of Law, and a BA from Brandeis University. He is admitted to practice law in the State of New York. Prior to this appointment as assistant director of ACDA, Dr. Scheinman served as president of Twenty-first Century Industries, Incorporated.

Dr. W. Andrew Terrill is a senior international security analyst at the Lawrence Livermore National Laboratory (LLNL). Dr. Terrill also served as a visiting professor of international security studies at the US Air War College at Maxwell Air Force Base, Alabama, from August 1998 until August 1999. At LLNL, Dr. Terrill specializes in the study of regional arms control and the proliferation of weapons of mass destruction in the Middle East. Since 1994, Dr. Terrill has been a frequent participant in the Arms Control and Regional Security Track 2 talks associated with the Middle East peace process. Dr. Terrill received his MA in political science from the University of California in 1976 and his PhD in international relations from Claremont Graduate University, Claremont, California, in 1983.

Index

1975 Biological and Toxin Weapon Convention: 1
1978 Camp David Accords: 114
1979 Egyptian–Israeli Peace Treaty: 114–15
1991 Gulf War: 124
1995 NPT Review and Extension Conference: 8
1997 Chemical Weapons Convention: 1

ACRS: 8, 82–83, 86–88, 90, 92, 117–18, 129
ACRS Track II: 129
active and passive defense: 15
active defenses: 16
Afghanistan: 40
American foreign policy: 80
Arab states: 64
Arab strategic environment: 62
arms control: 8, 83, 87, 89, 92, 94–96, 98–99, 109
arms control and regional security: 8
Arms Control and Regional Security Working Group: 82
arms race: 32
asymmetry: 88

Baker, James: 86
Bar–Lev, Chaim: 113
Barak, Ehud: 99
Bush administration: 96
Bushehr power reactor: 9

Camp David Accords: 115
chemical weapons attack: 15
Chemical Weapons Convention: 117, 129
Cheney, Richard: 124

denuclearization: 67
Desert Storm: 13
deterrence: 14, 19
discrimination: 69
dual containment: 35

Egypt: 7–8, 73, 85, 88, 91, 109, 112, 118, 123, 125
Egyptian domestic politics: 126
Elazar, David: 113

Fahmy, Nabil: 125
fissile material: 96, 98
Fissile Material Cutoff Treaty: 96–97

global nonproliferation regimes: 19
global regimes: 17
Gulf Cooperation Council: 30
Gulf War: 13, 31, 42

Hussein, King ibn Talal: 51, 123
Hussein, Saddam: 13, 42, 46, 79

International Atomic Energy Agency: 1, 18, 29, 85
Iran: 5, 10, 29–30, 33, 36–41, 49, 56, 71, 92–93
Iran–Iraq War: 29
Iranian Revolutionary Guard Corps: 37, 40
Iraq: 4, 9, 13, 29, 32–33, 36–37, 39, 42, 46–47, 50, 52–55, 57, 71, 79–80, 92–94, 115
Iraq's land forces: 43
Iraqi conventional missile attacks: 124
Iraqi Osiraq reactor project: 94
Israel: 4, 8, 12, 51, 69–70, 77, 81, 85, 89–91, 94, 97, 99, 110, 120, 124
Israeli Atomic Energy Commission: 113
Israeli nuclear capabilities: 100, 114
Israeli nuclear option: 71
Israeli nuclear program: 128
Israeli nuclear weapons: 111, 116, 118

Jordan: 51

Karem, Mahmoud: 113
Khatami, Mohammed: 30
Kuwait: 13, 44–46
Kuwaiti armed forces: 44

Lebanon: 122
Libya: 7

Madrid Peace Conference: 82, 86
Meir, Golda: 113
Middle East Peace Process: 8, 117
Middle Eastern security: 61
military balance: 29, 31
military expenditures: 33

Missile Technology and Control Regime:
    2
Mordecai, Vannunu: 115
Moussa, Amre: 116, 121–22, 125,
    127–28
MTCR: 10
Mubarak, Hosni: 116
Mubarak Initiative: 116, 121–22, 126–28

Nasser, Gamel Abdel: 110, 127
Ne'eman, Yuval: 113
Netanyahu, Benyamin: 99, 122, 127–128
nondiscrimination: 68
Nonproliferation Treaty of Nuclear
    Weapons: 1, 101, 119–21, 123,
    125–26
NPT Extension Conference: 119, 129
NPT Review Conference: 119
nuclear age: 78
nuclear arms control: 102, 110
nuclear capability: 71, 88
nuclear issue: 89, 95, 99
nuclear nonproliferation: 109
Nuclear Nonproliferation Treaty: 84, 109
nuclear option: 100
nuclear program: 94
nuclear proliferation: 80
nuclear reactor: 110
nuclear weapons: 66, 68, 73, 90–91, 93,
    96, 101, 111, 115, 117
nuclear weapons issues: 128
nuclear–armed adversary: 12
NWFZ: 69, 72–73, 84–85, 90, 95

opacity: 89, 91

peace process: 61, 92
peace treaty: 98
Pelindaba Treaty: 129
Peres, Shimon: 118–19, 121
political liberalization: 72
preposition: 45
proliferation: 1–2, 11, 13, 32, 40
proxy wars: 52

Rabin, Yitzhak: 121
Rafsanjani, Hashemi: 5
regimes: 16–18
regional architecture: 95

regional security: 83
Republican Guard: 43

Saudi Arabia: 34, 44–45
Scud missiles: 112
security assistance: 35
security policies: 19
security threats: 64
Segev, Samuel: 115
Shi'ite religious regime: 40
Sinai II agreement of 1975: 114
Southern Gulf: 31
Southern Gulf forces: 30
Southern Gulf military expenditures: 33
Soviet nuclear weapons: 112
Soviets: 112
strategic balance: 124
strategic issues: 124
Sunni tribal elites: 46
Syria: 6, 10, 98

tactical technology: 31
Taliban regime: 40
terrorism: 58, 71
terrorist organizations: 65
Tlas, Mustafa: 123
Turkey: 52
Tuwaitha reactor: 115

UN sanctions: 35
UN Security Council: 18
unconventional forces: 53
unconventional warfare: 41, 53
United Nations Special Commission: 5,
    29
United States: 12–15, 40, 45, 54–55
UNSCOM: 79
UNSCOM inspection: 92
US Central Command: 35
US power projection capabilities: 31

virtual nuclear arsenal: 100–01
virtual nuclear weapons: 102

weapons of mass destruction: 8–10,
    13–14, 16, 37, 49, 78–79, 93
weapons of mass destruction free zone:
    80, 88, 90, 95, 116
WMD programs: 94